# Trends in
# Organizational Behavior

## Volume 7
## TIME IN ORGANIZATIONAL BEHAVIOR

# Trends in Organizational Behavior

## Volume 7

## TIME IN ORGANIZATIONAL BEHAVIOR

Edited by

### Cary L. Cooper

Manchester School of Management, University of Manchester Institute of
Science and Technology, UK

and

### Denise M. Rousseau

Carnegie Mellon University, Pittsburgh, USA

## JOHN WILEY & SONS, LTD

Chichester · New York · Weinheim · Brisbane · Singapore · Toronto

*Trends in Organizational Behavior, Volume 7*

Published as a supplement to the *Journal of Organizational Behavior, Volume 21*

*Other Wiley Editorial Offices*

John Wiley & Sons, Inc., 605 Third Avenue,
New York, NY 10158-0012, USA

Wiley-VCH Verlag GmbH, Pappelallee 3,
D-69469 Weinheim, Germany

Jacaranda Wiley Ltd, 33 Park Road, Milton,
Queensland 4064, Australia

John Wiley & Sons (Asia) Pte Ltd, 2 Clementi Loop #02-01,
Jin Xing Distripark, Singapore 129809

John Wiley & Sons (Canada) Ltd, 22 Worcester Road,
Rexdale, Ontario M9W 1L1, Canada

**British Library Cataloguing in Publication Data**

A catalogue record for this book is available from the British Library

ISBN 0-471-49651-0

Typeset in 10/12 pt Palatino by Dorwyn Ltd, Rowlands Castle, Hants.
Printed and bound in Great Britain by Bookcraft (Bath) Ltd, Midsomer Norton.
This book is printed on acid-free paper responsibly manufactured from sustainable forestry, in which at least two trees are planted for each one used in paper production.

# Contents

# About the Editors

## CARY L. COOPER

Currently BUPA Professor of Organizational Psychology and Health at the Manchester School of Management (UMIST) and Pro-Vice-Chancellor of the University of Manchester Institute of Science and Technology. Professor Cooper is the author of over 80 books (on stress, women at work, and industrial and organizational psychology), has written over 250 articles for academic journals, and is a frequent contributor to national newspapers, TV and radio. He is President of the British Academy of Management, Founding Editor of the *Journal of Organizational Behavior*, and a Fellow of the British Psychological Society, the Royal Society of Arts, the Royal Society of Medicine, Royal Society of Health, the Academy of Management and the British Academy of Management. He is also Co-Editor, with Chris Argyris, of the twelve-volume *Encyclopedia of Management* (Blackwell); and Co-Editor of *Stress Medicine* and the *International Journal of Management Reviews*.

## DENISE M. ROUSSEAU

Denise Rousseau H. J. Heinz II Professor of Organizational Behavior and Public Policy at Carnegie Mellon University, jointly in the Heinz School of Public Policy and Management and in the Graduate School of Industrial Administration. She has been a faculty member at Northwestern University, the University of Michigan, and the Naval Postgraduate School.

Her research addresses the impact of work group processes on performance and the changing psychological contract at work. Rousseau is an author of more than 80 articles which have appeared in prominent academic journals, such as the *Journal of Applied Psychology*, *Academy of Management Review*, and *Administrative Science Quarterly*. She is currently Editor-in-Chief of the *Journal of Organizational Behavior*. Her other books include: *Psychological Contracts in Organizations: Understanding Written and*

*Unwritten Agreements* (Sage); the *Trends in Organizational Behavior* series (Wiley) with Cary Cooper, *Developing an Interdisciplinary Science of Organizations* (Jossey-Bass) with Karlene Roberts and Charles Hulin; *The Boundaryless Career* (Oxford) with Michael Arthur; *Psychological Contracts in Employment: Cross-National Perspectives* (Sage, 2000) with Rene Schalk; and *Relational Wealth* (Oxford, 2000) with Carrie Leana.

Professor Rousseau has consulted in diverse organizations and written numerous articles for managers and executives including "Teamwork: inside and out" (*Business Week/Advance*), "Managing diversity for high performance" (*Business Week/Advance*) and "Two ways to change (and keep) the psychological contract" (*Academy of Management Executive*). She has taught in executive programs at Northwestern (Kellogg), Cornell, Carnegie Mellon and in industry programs for health care, journalism and manufacturing among others.

She is a Fellow in the American Psychological Association, Society for Industrial and Organizational Psychology, and the Academy of Management.

# List of Contributors

Stuart Albert

Carlson School of Management, 3–365, University of Minnesota, 321 19th Avenue South, Minneapolis, MN 55455, USA

Michelle L. Buck

Faculty of Management, McGill University, 1001 Sherbrooke Street West, Montreal, Quebec H3A 1G5, Canada

Kevin G. Corley

403 Beam BAB, Penn State University, University Park, PA 16802, USA

Tommaso Fabbri

University of Modena, 41100, Modena, Italy

Dennis A. Gioia

403 Beam BAB, Penn State University, University Park, PA 16802, USA

Cherlyn Skromme Granrose

Campbell School of Business, Berry College, MT. Berry, GA 30149, USA

Jeffrey H. Greenhaus

Department of Management, Le Bow College of Business, Drexel University, Philadelphia, PA 19104, USA

Catherine Kirchmeyer

School of Business Administration, Wayne State University, Detroit, MI 48202, USA

Mary Dean Lee

Faculty of Management, McGill University, 1001 Sherbrooke Street West, Montreal, Quebec H3A 1G5, Canada

Frank Linnehan

Department of Management, Le Bow College of Business, Drexel University, Philadelphia, PA 19104, USA

Shelley MacDermid

Purdue University, 504 Northwestern Avenue, West Lafayette, IN 47907, USA

*Saroj Parasuraman*        Department of Management, Le Bow
                           College of Business, Drexel University,
                           Philadelphia, PA 19104, USA

*Stephen Smith*            Purdue University, 504 Northwestern
                           Avenue, West Lafayette, IN 47907, USA

*Mary J. Waller*           Department of Business Administration,
                           University of Illinois at Urbana-
                           Champaign, 1206 South 6th Street,
                           Champaign, IL 61820, USA

*Akbar Zaheer*             Carlson School of Management, 3–365,
                           University of Minnesota, 321 19th Avenue
                           South, Minneapolis, MN 55455, USA

*Srilata Zaheer*           Carlson School of Management, 3–365,
                           University of Minnesota, 321 19th Avenue
                           South, Minneapolis, MN 55455, USA

# Editorial Introduction

Fill in the blank: "Time is _____." Having asked this question of our classes for years, we find that people's answers vary—by country of origin (time is money to our UK- and US-born students and anything from "life", "a circle", to a "a journey" for those from Africa and Southeast Asia) or whether they aspire to be business people or poets. The arrival of the millennium (does it start this year or next?) has raised consciousness regarding time and its meaning.

This volume of *Trends in Organizational Behavior* focuses on time in organizational behavior. Conceptions of time are human-made. Zaheer, Albert & Zaheer examine both organizational and researcher-derived time scales and their impact on our understanding of organizational behavior. Cross-cultural perspectives on time have been addressed in a variety of disciplines but Granrose takes these one step further by addressing cross-cultural conceptions of time in careers. Parasuraman, Greenhaus & Linnehan model career transitions from different time perspectives and their connection to person–career fit. The interplay of the demands of personal and organizational time raises issues associated with viewing time as a resource (somewhere between "money" and "life"). This interplay generates reflections and tough decisions among the professionals and managers whom Buck *et al.* describe in their chapter on reduced workloads. Kirchmeyer offers a critical look at this interplay by addressing the organizational motives at the heart of many corporate work–life initiatives. Lastly, with a fluid view of time, less a scarce resource and more like an emerging process, Corley, Gioia & Fabbri portray the malleability of organizational identity over time. We believe readers will find personal and professional insights as well as intellectual ones.

DMR
CLC

# CHAPTER 1

# The Importance of Time Scales

Srilata Zaheer, Stuart Albert and Akbar Zaheer

*Carlson School of Management, University of Minnesota, USA*

## INTRODUCTION

The Chinese leader Mao Zedong was once asked what he thought of the French Revolution. He is reported to have answered, "It's too early to say." This seemingly flip reply raises an important question: over what time frames can phenomena be understood or evaluated? The issue is significant in organizational life as well where some actions can play out in a matter of seconds; others may unfold over years. So too the consequences of actions. The meaning of an action and its consequences often depend on the time scale over which they are manifested. Thus, your boss' momentary frown after lunch could simply signal indigestion. If it persists for a week or more, then you might think of dusting off your résumé. As a general rule, crises tend to focus attention on the most immediate, and hence force one to react at micro-level time scales. In the process, actions that have a longer life span may be ignored or missed, or underweighted in one's responses. For example, a fall in the *Business Week* rankings of a graduate school might divert attention from crucial initiatives that might be in the works for years, in favor of superficial quick fixes that lose their effectiveness in a matter of weeks. All of these examples have to do with different types of *time scales* over which actions, events, processes, phenomena, and their implications are played out. These include time scales that managers and researchers use to make sense of their worlds and to chart the course of phenomena of interest.

By time scales we mean the levels of differentiation of a temporal continuum, objectively or subjectively defined, that are used by managers

*Trends in Organizational Behavior*, Volume 7. Edited by C. L. Cooper and D. M. Rousseau.
Copyright © 2000 John Wiley & Sons, Ltd.

or researchers to define, observe, measure, or interpret phenomena of interest. Some phenomena are best understood using time scale "lenses" of weeks rather than seconds or years—other phenomena may be most "in focus" over time scales of months. At a certain level of temporal magnification, certain patterns will be visible or salient, while others will not. The key is using the *appropriate* time scale, i.e. that which highlights the essential elements of the phenomenon of interest or those of its consequences.

We wish to distinguish our use of the concept of time scales from colloquial usage in which the granularity of time scale is used to speak of rate of change or speed. For example, if someone says, "It takes only a few seconds" or, "It'll take years", they are often referring to the *speed* at which some process unfolds. In our definition, the second or the year represents instead the temporal unit that is needed to define and see the process with clarity. We also do not discuss the roles of time *per se*, in organizations.[1] We assume, although we will not develop this notion, that for any given process there is a range of time scales that will reveal the features in which one is interested. At more macro or more micro time scales, other features may well be revealed, but not the ones of focal interest. Thus, the choice of time scale determines what one sees and what one believes to be important.

While there are many ways to categorize time scales, we find it helpful to think in terms of the practical use to which time scales are put. In the process of understanding phenomena and the relationships between them, the first important time scale to consider is what we term the "existence interval". By the existence interval we mean the length of time needed for one instance of the phenomenon in question to occur or unfold; an interval that corresponds to the life span of the phenomenon. Other time scales can be defined that describe the temporal intervals researchers or managers use to think about and analyze the phenomena in question. An "observation interval" defines the period over which a phenomenon is observed in order to understand it. A "recording interval" is the frequency at which the properties of a phenomenon are captured or recorded. An "aggregation interval" is the time scale over which the recorded information is aggregated. For example, data may be collected every second (recording interval), for a month (observation interval), and aggregated for analytic purposes at hourly intervals (aggregation interval). A circadian rhythm, with repeating patterns of ebbs and flows during the course of an organizational workday, might only become evident when using an existence interval of 24 hours.

---

[1] See Bluedorn & Denhardt (1988) or Clark (1985) for a general review of theories of time in organizations, and Kelley & McGrath (1988) for further discussion of methodological issues.

Another kind of time scale is the "validity interval", which describes the temporal interval over which relationships between phenomena hold.[2] The validity interval is an important concept because it defines the time scale of cause and effect—action and reaction—of implicit or explicit theories with which managers and researchers live and work. Furthermore, every organizational process, insofar as it unfolds in time, has a time scale or scales associated with it. For example, there is an "existence interval" associated with performance evaluation in firms. This evaluation existence interval is likely to vary across firms, industries, and professions. Managers moving from one industry to another, such as from commercial banking to an internet-based industry, need to recognize and adjust their implicit and explicit evaluation existence intervals to the far more compressed evaluation existence intervals operating in the internet world.

Issues that surround time scales share some features in common with issues concerning levels of analysis in organizational research (Rousseau 1985). Concepts that apply at the firm level may not apply at the individual level of analysis. Phenomena that are important on a monthly basis may be irrelevant at longer or shorter time scales. A decade-long capital campaign may have little relevance for resource availability on a day-to-day basis. Similarly, the pressure to meet annual budgets may not translate well into pressure to meet a daily budget. Furthermore, in organizational research, the individual and the firm levels of analysis often have a privileged position, just as the micro-scale of the present moment and perhaps the macro-scale of the remaining life span tend to be central temporal foci.

In this chapter, we introduce the notion of time scales using a specific empirical example with actual time-series data, which illustrates the implications for relationships between variables when they are examined at different time scales. We then discuss the implications of time scales for research and for managerial practice.

## AN ILLUSTRATION OF THE EFFECTS OF TIME SCALE

Managers are constantly trying to understand their worlds—to make sense of what is happening to their business units, what their competitors are doing, or how environmental trends are affecting demand. A key managerial task is to make sense of change, and to understand how changes in one phenomenon are related to changes in others. But how

---

[2] For a full exposition of these types of time scales and their roles in theory development, see Zaheer, Albert & Zaheer (1999).

much change is occurring is a function of the time scale one is using to examine and understand the phenomenon. Selecting inappropriate time scales over which to examine phenomena of interest could lead to one missing the fact that the phenomena are correlated, or, at the other extreme, observing a correlation that may not be important for the time frame over which decisions have to be made. For example, while threats can lead to a short-term increase in productivity, the continued use of threat is likely to lead to the reverse: subject to continuous high levels of threat, the best people are likely to exit. If the effects of threat on productivity were being examined over a short time frame, managers could come to erroneous conclusions about the effectiveness of threat. Conventional wisdom already distinguishes between the fact that what works in the short run may not work in the long run, and vice versa. However, highlighting the importance of time scales is to make a subtly different point: that, quite literally, the relationships one "sees", and the actions triggered by those observations, depend critically on the time scales one is using.

Consider an example from our research in financial markets (Zaheer & Zaheer 1997). A manager of a brokerage firm is trying to understand how volatility in the market will impact the volume of trades flowing into her unit in order to decide on the resources that she needs to allocate to the order-processing function. She therefore needs to understand the nature of the relationship between volatility and the volume of orders. If she uses an inappropriate time scale to assess the correlation between volatility and order flow, then she may miss the connection entirely, or underweight its importance.

We have actual time-series data on a related phenomenon linking two variables, volatility in currency prices, and the flow of inquiries marketwide, for a single day in the currency markets. The global currency trading industry is interesting in that its operating cycle is known to be extremely short—in as little as 3 min, information is collected and processed, deals are consummated, and profits and losses (sometimes large) taken (Lyons 1993). Moreover, data are available on a continuous, real-time basis, raising the question of the appropriate temporal unit of analysis for studying processes in this marketplace. A brief description of the industry context and the data and methods used is given in the appendix at the end of this chapter.

We selected three time scales (aggregation intervals) at which we aggregated the data: 10 sec, 2 min, and 5 min. At first glance, it would appear that since data are available second-by-second for both variables of interest, data at this most precise level, or aggregation interval, should be used to understand the relationship between volatility and order flows. However, the question of what second-by-second volatility means is raised immediately. While this industry is known to have extremely short cycles—as mentioned above, 3 min is a long time in currency trading—the idea of changing volatility every *second* seems to be clearly absurd. Simply put, organizational responses to environmental phenomena imply human agency and cognitive and physical limitations that preclude adjustments to volatility every single second. As a result, we used our judgment to select the three time scales at which to examine the relationships, one substantially smaller than, one close to, and one substantially larger than the typical 3 min operating cycle in this industry (Callier, 1986).

The time scale (aggregation interval) chosen to aggregate the phenomena and examine the link between market volatility and order flow clearly makes a difference to their statistical relationship, as can be seen from Figure 1.1. In fact, the relationship between order flows and volatility is dramatically affected by the choice of the aggregation interval time scale. The correlation coefficient increases from 0.31 to 0.71 and further to a sizable 0.81 as the time scale increases from 10 s to 2 and 5 min. The differences in these correlations are significant at the 0.01 level. A theory of a close relationship between market volatility in currency prices and the flow of orders is therefore only weakly supported at an aggregation interval time scale of 10 s, but is rather strongly borne out at an aggregation interval time scale of 5 min, when the correlation between the variables is a high 0.81. While we do not elaborate on the theory underlying the relationship here, our point is merely that the nature of the relationship itself can change quite dramatically, depending on the choice of the aggregation interval. In brief, what you see depends on what time scale you use.

## DISCUSSION

### Managing in Multiple Time Scales

In discussing the implications of time scales, an important point is to be cognizant of the multiple time scales in use. For example, going back to the performance evaluation example mentioned earlier, we suggest that evaluation is an inherently multi-time-scale process, while it is not often recognized as such. Some professions, such as the US presidency, or the CEO of a company, are under continuous evaluation, which is evaluation at the finest time-scale available. At the same time, a president is judged at the end of his first 100 days, at the end of his first term, and decades after he leaves office. A company's stock price is a daily "report card" on the CEO's performance, quarterly earnings provide quarterly evaluations, and the annual report is a time for the stockholders and the market to assess CEO performance over the course of the year just ended. One

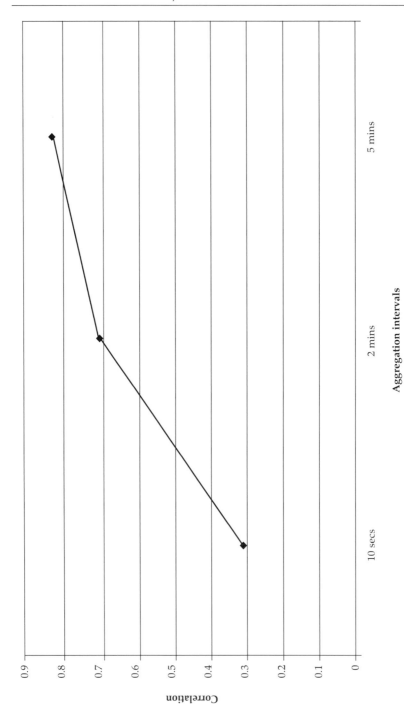

**Figure 1.1**   Correlation between volatility and order flows at different time scales

implication of the presence of multiple time scales for evaluation may be that the individual being evaluated needs to match performance existence intervals with evaluation existence intervals, such as by delivering up "small successes" as well as "large successes".

In fact, the whole point of historical judgment is to assert the value of a macro time scale. This is not to give primacy to macro over micro time scales, since there are many occasions where a more micro time scale may be essential. For example, it is important to recognize and reward immediately an unusually difficult achievement. Organizations whose reward and evaluation systems only operate at fixed macro time scales risk "missing the moment". Managers who recognize and appreciate the multiplicity of time scales, and implicitly or explicitly apply appropriate time scales to relevant phenomena, are more likely to be effective.

## Empty Intervals and Lost Information

One of the consequences of a manager selecting a very fine time scale is the inevitable presence of the empty interval and the crucial task of interpreting its meaning. At finer intervals, one will inevitably face some time periods where the phenomenon of interest is absent. Does the absence of a competitive response within one week of a new product introduction mean that the competition is unaware, is not going to respond, is unprepared, or is simply getting ready for a bigger response? The manager will have to interpret the meaning of the missing data or the empty interval, just as one has to interpret the meaning of silences (Picard 1964; Albert 1980, 1995).

On the other side, going to a more and more macro time scale may cause you to lose important information on the sequence of events, which may be fundamental to understanding cause–effect relationships. There is also the danger of losing information that is only disclosed at a more micro time scale. For instance, if a manager only collected information on a competitor's prices once a quarter, she might miss the fact that the competitor was matching the firm's price movements throughout the quarter.

## The Costs of Time Scale Choice

While it may seem wise to select a recording interval time scale that is as fine as possible, such a choice is not entirely costless. For example, if a manager decided she needed to obtain intelligence about a competitor's actions on a daily basis, then the cost would be substantially higher than monitoring their visible actions that may be disclosed only monthly or quarterly. The choice of time scales has to be driven by a combination of the phenomena of interest, the cost of obtaining information, and the manager's strategy in terms of what the manager plans to do with the understanding she gets from examining the relationships involved. It would be an error to assume that finer time scales always yield better information, because finer time scales inevitably run up against the interpretive difficulties of the empty interval. One may be unable to use very fine-grained information if it results in many empty intervals that one does not have a theory to interpret. Thus one should be aware of one's biases about time scales. A historian would do well to examine phenomena at a finer time scale than she might normally use, just as an accountant might gain some insights from examining information over longer historical spans.

## Strategy and Time Scales

All business and corporate strategies presuppose time scales. The increased concern with developing business strategies in "internet time", whereby a firm like Netscape has had to reinvent itself thrice in a two-year period (Prahalad 1999), suggests that the time scale over which strategies have to be formulated and implemented may be different across different industries. Furthermore, the time scales may be shrinking as we cross the millennium.

In our trading example, different trading strategies presuppose different time scales. For example, the strategy of a day trader would differ from that of a trader that buys to hold, and the level of volatility monitored by these different traders would depend on the time scale chosen. As we have emphasized, the ability to "see" a pattern in data is determined by the time scale, and this in turn determines the trading strategy that one can use to exploit the phenomenon.

Increasingly, firms have to confront the fact that different business units have strategies that make different time scales salient. Boeing may build and sell jets for which the time scale of relevance may be in years (note that the speed at which Boeing builds jets is likely to have only a limited impact on the length of this time scale). Performance evaluation and rewards may be entrained (Ancona & Chong 1996) to the operating cycle of building a jet. If Boeing were involved in a different activity, say, in running an internet-based service operation, then it would be likely to need to use a very different time scale to measure performance in that activity, and to understand the market for that activity.

## The Integration of Multiple Time Scales

This brings us to a fundamental problem confronting most organizations—the need to coordinate activities that operate across multiple time scales. We give below some suggestions on how firms might approach this problem.

The simplest solution is to only operate at one time scale, and eliminate or separate activities that cannot be entrained (Ancona & Chong 1996) to the dominant time scale. Of course, such efforts are likely to result in the loss of potential synergies across activities that operate under different time scales. Alternatively, firms need to invent a "differential"—a mechanism that allows for coupling asynchronous time scales. This may, for instance, take the form of an institutionalized process, say, in the strategic planning system, that forces managers to pay attention to a range of time scales.

Another option is to train managers to think along multiple time scales by, say, rotating them through positions that require thinking and decision-making along time scales of different lengths. Managers' evaluation and reward time scales can also be manipulated to force them to think and act in a time frame to which they are unaccustomed.

## CONCLUSION

In managers' preoccupation with speed as a source of competitive advantage (Eisenhardt 1989; Nayyar & Bantel, 1994), there is a danger of missing the fact that it is not only about doing things faster, but it is also about seeing useful patterns and developing strategies based on them. The critical issue that we emphasize in this chapter is not that longer time scales are necessarily better or worse than shorter time scales, but that different phenomena and processes are best understood at different time scales. To see a pattern may require thinking about, observing, and measuring a phenomenon at a time scale different from that to which one is accustomed. In this chapter, we take a first step toward calling managers' attention to the importance of time scales in making sense of processes in their organizations and their environments.

## APPENDIX

### Data and Methods

Data on the *order flows* on the global electronic dealing system were obtained from Reuters. Roughly 4000 banks are present on the database. The data are a complete record of activity in the currency market for roughly 10 h on 4 September, 1994. A total of 176 000 incoming calls, which represent order inquiries, are recorded on the database, on a second-by-second basis.

A second publicly available database, the High Frequency Data in Finance (HFDF), was used for the price-quote data advertised on the Reuters Monitor. Dollar–mark prices (prices of dollars in marks) are available from the public Reuters Monitor, also time-stamped to the nearest second. These are indicative prices at which a bank is prepared to deal a standard lot of currency (typically US$5 million). We used this price quote data to construct a measure of *market volatility*. Employing a standard finance operationalization (Ito, Lyons & Melvin 1998), we calculated the log difference between the highest bid prices quoted in successive time periods. If prices were missing in either of the successive time periods, then we defined volatility to be equal to zero. In doing this, we work with an implicit theory about the meaning of missing price data within a time interval of a particular size (the empty interval). Volatility was calculated for the same three chosen measurement intervals. The measures of order flows and volatility were aggregated at successive 10 s, 2 min and 5 min measurement intervals.

## ACKNOWLEDGMENTS

All authors contributed equally to this chapter. The order of authorship was decided by random drawing.

## REFERENCES

Albert, S. (1980) Dynamics and paradoxes of the ending process. In S. Albert & E. C. Luck (Eds), *On the Endings of Wars* (pp. 9–24). New York: Kennikat Press.
Albert, S. (1995) Towards a theory of timing: an archival study of timing decisions in the Persian Gulf war. In B. M. Staw & L. L. Cummings (Eds), *Research in Organizational Behavior* (Vol. 17, pp. 1–69). Greenwich, CT: JAI Press.
Ancona, D. & Chong, C-L. (1996) Entrainment: pace, cycle, and rhythm in organizational behavior. In B. M. Staw & L. L. Cummings (Eds), *Research in Organizational Behavior* (Vol. 18, pp. 251–284). Greenwich, CT: JAI Press.
Bluedorn, A. C. & Denhardt, R. B. (1988) Time and organizations. *Journal of Management*, **14**(2): 299–320.
Callier, P. (1986) 'Professional trading', Exchange rate risk and the growth of international banking—a note, *Banca Nazionale del Lavoro Quarterly Review*, **159**: 423–428.
Clark, P. (1985) A review of the theories of time and structure for orgnizational sociology. *Research in the Sociology of Organizations*, **4**: 35–79.
Eisenhardt, K. (1989) Making fast strategic decisions in high-velocity environments. *Academy of Management Journal*, **32**(3): 543–576.
Ito, T., Lyons, R. K., and Melvin, M. T. (1998) Is there private information in the FX market? The Tokyo Experiment. *Journal of Finance*, **53**: 1111–1130.
Kelley, J. R. & McGrath, J. E. (1988) *On Time and Method*. Newbury Park, CA: Sage.

Lyons, R. K. (1993) Tests of microstructural hypothesis in the foreign exchange market. *Journal of Financial Economics*, **39**: 321–351.

Nayyar, P. R. & Bantel, K. A. (1994) Competitive agility: a source of competitive advantage based on speed and variety. In P. Shrivastava, A. S. Huff & J. E. Dutton (Eds), *Advances in Strategic Management: Resource-based View of the Firm*, (Vol. 10A, pp. 193–222). Greenwich, CT: JAI Press.

Picard, M. (1964) *The World of Silence*. Chicago: Henry Regnery.

Prahalad, C. K. (1999) The Market as a Forum. Strategic Management Research Center Colloquium delivered at the Carlson School of Management, University of Minnesota, 15 October, 1999.

Rousseau, D. M. (1985) Issues of level in organizational research: multi-level and cross-level perspectives. In B. M. Staw & L. L. Cummings (Eds), *Research in Organizational Behavior*, (Vol. 7, pp. 1–37). Greenwich, CT: JAI Press.

Zaheer, A. & Zaheer, S. (1997) Catching the wave: alertness, responsiveness and market influence in global electronic networks. *Management Science,* **43**(11): 1493–1509.

Zaheer, S., Albert, S. & Zaheer, A. (1999). Time scales and organizational theory. *Academy of Management Review*, **24**(4): 725–741.

CHAPTER 2

# Reduced-load Work and the Experience of Time among Professionals and Managers: Implications for Personal and Organizational Life

Michelle L. Buck and Mary Dean Lee
*McGill University, Canada*

and

Shelley M. MacDermid and Stephen Smith
*Purdue University, USA*

## INTRODUCTION

Living in today's fast-paced world, many employees are finding their work life and career to be all-consuming (Babbar & Aspelin 1998; Schor 1991). In a recent survey, 50 per cent of respondents felt that they spent "too much time" working or thinking about work (*Fast Company*–Roper Starch Worldwide Online Survey, 1999, p. 214). Twenty-seven per cent of respondents said that they spent 6–10 hours a week "thinking about [their] job—while doing other, non-work activities", and an additional 20 per cent of respondents said they spent 11 or more hours each week doing the same (p. 220). The actual number of hours spent working is steadily increasing as well (Bond, Galinsky & Swanberg 1998; Moen 1999). According to a recent Statistics Canada survey, time spent in the

*Trends in Organizational Behavior*, Volume 7. Edited by C. L. Cooper and D. M. Rousseau.
Copyright © 2000 John Wiley & Sons, Ltd.

workplace has increased by two hours a week every year since 1992 (*Montreal Gazette* 1999). While often highly committed to professional achievement and willing to expend long hours and energy to succeed and advance, many workers simultaneously feel pulled in other directions as well. Managers and professionals are increasingly likely to be part of dual career or single parent families, managing both career and family responsibilities. Many workers are not only facing decisions about childcare arrangements, but also investing time and energy in care for elderly parents. More individuals are focused on balancing personal time and personal well-being with professional development and career success. Meanwhile, at work, many employees in the post-downsizing era face scenarios in which organizations are trying to get more work done by fewer people. The Statistics Canada survey reports that one-third of Canadians, aged 25 to 44, identified themselves as workaholics (Tobin 1999), over half said that they did not have enough time for family or friends, and almost as many said that they felt "trapped in a daily routine" (*Montreal Gazette* 1999). Workers are often feeling frustrated by the inconsistency between the reality of their harried lives and a vision of comfortably balancing the multiple roles, interests, responsibilities, and motivations of their lives.

People are responding to these pressures in a variety of ways. This chapter intends to explore some of the issues relating to employees' attempts to manage multiple priorities in their lives. More specifically, it will look at cases from a recent study of high-ranking professionals and managers who are voluntarily working part-time for family and lifestyle reasons (see Lee & MacDermid *et al.* 1998), and examine some of the individual and organizational outcomes of reducing the number of hours spent at work. The chapter will conclude by considering broader implications of redesigning the way work is done and the way time is distributed between work life and personal life: what is the impact upon some traditional management practices, such as using face time as an indicator of commitment, or providing standard vs. customized compensation packages? How does the allocation of time, and perceptions of choice about time use, influence workers' *experience* of time? And what is the relationship between the experience of time and personal identity? That is, how does time use influence how workers feel about themselves and how they are able to express themselves?

The cases of part-time professionals and managers are just one part of a broad mosaic of responses to the conflicting demands of work and personal life. People are pursuing or designing alternative work arrangements that involve creative options of how and where they spend their time, and seeking greater freedom and flexibility in how their time is allocated between work and non-work life (Catalyst 1997;

Epstein *et al.* 1998; Mirchandani, 1998; Scandura & Lankau, 1997). In the media and in personal anecdotes and conversations, we hear an echoing refrain of frustration with the status quo of long hours, heavy workload, and mounting stress, and an eagerness, almost a yearning, for a different way of doing things that somehow captures a sense of wholeness, of value, and satisfaction. A recent issue of *Fast Company* magazine (July–August 1999) was devoted to exploring, "How to design a life that works", and features several articles on individuals' search to integrate different parts of their lives and find a greater sense of well-being. A recent book, *When Work Doesn't Work Anymore* (McKenna 1997), chronicles the journeys of women who "wanted more than conventional success, . . . who wanted a life too" (p. 9) and find that "the only answer becomes working differently and under very different conditions" (p. 37).

Many workers are experiencing frustration, yet feel unable to initiate change for fear of risking the stability of the jobs they have, either because of the apparently limited possibilities of something different, or due to the built-in incentives of working long hours. For example, the income sharing that characterizes legal partnerships creates an incentive to promote associates who have the capacity to work very hard, and a large number of billable hours is often used as the indicator of this propensity to work hard (Landers, Rebitzer & Taylor 1996). Bailyn (1994) comments that, in other settings, lower-level workers in organizations may be reluctant to explore alternatives to traditional job design and career paths because they see no higher-level employees pursuing such arrangements.

Despite potential constraints or lack of precedent, some workers are indeed beginning to experiment with a variety of alternative arrangements as a means of attempting more effectively to manage the multiple priorities in their lives. Some workers are choosing to telecommute from home offices, allowing them to reduce commute times, be closer to family members, or better coordinate childcare arrangements. Others are choosing flextime as an option to fulfill similar goals, abandoning traditional hours and adopting a schedule that better accommodates events both away from and at the office. Some are reducing the numbers of hours worked each week, either by trying to cut back from 50- or 60-plus hour weeks, or by officially becoming part-time workers. Still others are abandoning the corporate world and its accompanying lifestyle entirely, opting for entrepreneurship as a means of increasing flexibility and perceived control in their lives. In all of these scenarios of alternative work arrangements, the common theme is the workers' efforts to change their working conditions, and the time spent in traditional organizational work settings, in order to create a different lifestyle, and have increased freedom and flexibility in how their time is spent.

We focus in particular upon the alternative work arrangements of managers and professionals who are working part-time, and receiving proportional reduced compensation. Part-time work has traditionally involved those who do not choose to work less, who are in lower-level jobs that are poorly compensated, and who receive no benefits. However, several recent research reports suggest increased numbers of professionals are seeking reduced-load, or part-time, work arrangements, and that the negative consequences associated with traditional part-time work do not necessarily apply (Catalyst 1997; Clark 1998; Lee & MacDermid *et al.* 1998; Lee & Smucker 1999; Levy, Flynn & Kellogg 1997; Meiksins & Whalley 1995). This category of arrangements is noteworthy because of the deviation it represents from traditional patterns of career development and professional expectations. Due to the workload and complex nature of work tasks and responsibilities, professionals are generally assumed to work long hours, frequently exceeding the official designation of 40 hours per week as a "full-time" position. The dedication required of a professional is assumed to involve a commitment to "do what it takes" to get the job done. Consequently, part-time work among professionals and managers, who are high-level, well-compensated employees, elicits questions about potential career risks (Ableson 1998; Epstein *et al.* 1998; Seron & Feiris 1995), but also generates opportunities to examine the changing nature of employment relations and career structures. By examining the ways in which professional jobs can be redesigned to accommodate a part-time schedule, and the impact of these arrangements upon individual and organizational outcomes, we simultaneously explore larger issues, such as: challenges to traditional notions of managing the workforce; ways in which employees use and experience time; and the link between the experience of time and personal identity.

## SAMPLE AND METHODOLOGY

A qualitative study of reduced-load, or part-time, work in the United States and Canada examined the cases of 82 managers and professionals working less than full-time (for example, working four days a week, rather than five) by choice, with an accompanying reduction in compensation, for family and/or lifestyle reasons.[1] The intent of the study was to document how these arrangements came to be, and how they were working out, from the perspective of multiple stakeholders. Each case included interviews with the target manager or professional, their senior manager, a peer-level co-worker, a spouse or partner, where applicable, and a human resources representative

---

[1] No systematic differences have been observed between the US and Canadian samples.

of the organization. By definition, managerial participants were those responsible for the work of three or more direct reports. The 46 managers in the study were project managers, line managers, or those responsible for managing professionals in a support function, such as Director of Finance. The 36 participants in professional-level jobs were individuals with specific expertise, knowledge, and skill who were functioning as individual contributors in their organizations, in areas such as research and development, marketing, engineering, finance, human resources, and communications.

Participants were recruited using a variety of strategies, including personal contacts with human resource and work/life administrators, "cold calls" to employers, and direct mail solicitations to members of organizations. We sought to include a wide range of cases along dimensions such as the type of job, the size and industry of the company, reasons for pursuing reduced-load work, and the degree of load reduction. Because there is no readily available sampling frame of individuals working reduced load and because this work arrangement is still relatively uncommon, our sampling methods were necessarily purposive and nonrandom. Based on existing estimates of the extent of men's participation in reduced-load work at the professional and managerial level (Catalyst 1997), we aimed for 10–20 per cent of our sample being men.

About 90 per cent of the respondents were female,[2] and about 90 per cent had children. Table 2.1 provides additional demographic

**Table 2.1**    Demographic Information—Target Employee Sample

|  | Professionals ($n = 36$) | Managers ($n = 46$) |
|---|---|---|
| % Female | 87% | 92% |
| Mean age | 39.5 | 38.3 |
| Mean salary (US$) | $48 576 | $63 535 |
| Mean spouse/partner salary (US$) | $70 577 | $93 167 |
| % with post-graduate degree | 58% | 45% |
| Mean no, yrs on reduced load | 4.76 | 3.79 |
| Mean per cent load reduction | 69% | 73% |
| Mean current hrs/week | 30 | 34 |
| Mean previous hrs/week | 49 | 51 |
| Mean yrs experience before red. load | 13.5 | 13.6 |
| Mean age of youngest child | 5.3 | 4.5 |
| Mean age of oldest child | 7.9 | 7.1 |

[2] The small number of men in the sample, and in reduced-load arrangements more generally, makes it difficult to find systematic differences between the male and female participants. However, it can be noted that the men in the sample were pursuing reduced load for more of a variety of reasons than the women: phasing into retirement, more time for leisure activities or religious activities, relief from highly stressful work, time for caring for an elderly parent, as well as for more time with children.

information about the sample. Interviews were conducted in 42 firms, representing a wide variety of industries and functional areas. No more than four cases of part-time professionals or managers came from any one firm. The appendix at the end of the chapter includes additional information about the industries represented. Although participating companies ranged in size from 170 to 240 000 employees, they were mostly quite large, averaging 48 000 workers. On average, their workforces were 46.4 per cent female, 15.6 per cent unionized, and 10.9 per cent part-time.

Managers and professionals who were parents reported that they pursued reduced-load arrangements in large part for family reasons. Those respondents without children typically requested reduced-load work either to achieve a greater sense of balance in their lives, allowing them to have time to pursue hobbies, religious activities, community service, or in response to concerns about their health. In most cases, participants were able significantly to reduce their amount of time at work to a mean of 32 hours a week, compared with a mean of 50 hours when they were full-time. Their reduced-load work arrangements had been in existence for about four years, on average, at the time of the study, and respondents were generally experienced in the firm, having been with their employer for a mean of 13 years.

Data were collected in one-on-one, confidential interviews with the target manager or professional, and with his or her spouse or partner, the target's senior manager, a peer co-worker, and a human resource representative from the company. Ninety per cent of the interviews were face-to-face, while the remainder took place on the telephone. The interviews with target respondents lasted about 1.5 hours; all other interviews lasted about 45 minutes. All interviews were audio-recorded and transcribed verbatim for analysis. Over 350 interviews were conducted in total. The interviews were semi-structured, including questions on the following topics:

- The structure of and reasons for the reduced-load work arrangement
- How the job was restructured to accommodate the reduced-load schedule
- Perceptions of the challenges and difficulties involved in restructuring the job
- Costs and benefits of reduced-load work from multiple perspectives
- Factors important in making the arrangements more successful or less successful

Interviews were conducted by a member of a team of seven researchers. Usually, one interviewer gathered all the data for a particular case. Data were gathered between August 1996 and March 1998.

In addition to the interviews with stakeholders, questionnaire surveys were sent to the direct reports of target managers in the sample, but these were completed anonymously. Of the 253 direct reports of the 46 managers in the study, 218 were sent questionnaires to be returned directly to the researchers.[3] Overall, 72 per cent ($n = 153$) of the surveys were returned, and in 22 cases this included 100 per cent of direct reports. In the survey, respondents indicated their assessment of the manager's overall effectiveness, and their level of agreement with statements about the effects of their manager's reduced-load work arrangement on (a) their own work experience; (b) their relationship with their boss; and (c) the work unit as a whole.

Following the collection of data for a particular case, the interviewer used interview transcripts, direct report questionnaires, and any personal field notes and observations to extract material related to pre-identified categories, including logistics and negotiations of the arrangement, pros and cons, facilitating and hindering factors of success, managerial strategies, gender ideology, organizational characteristics of the firm, and human resource policies. The interviewer then wrote a "reflective memo" to summarize main themes and to include a global rating of the overall success of the part-time arrangement. This overall success rating integrated the perspective of all stakeholders. First, the perspective of the target worker was considered: to what extent did they fulfill their objectives of going on reduced load, and how satisfied were they with the perceived benefits, relative to the perceived costs and tradeoffs, from personal and career perspectives? Secondly, the organizational perspective was evaluated in terms of the extent to which the senior manager, coworkers, and others in a work group reported positive outcomes. Thirdly, the family perspective considered the impact of the reduced-load work arrangement upon children, family life, and/or the couple's relationship. Finally, we examined the consistency across all stakeholders in all three perspectives in reporting positive or negative consequences of the work arrangement. On a scale of 1 to 9, a "1" indicated consistently negative outcomes reported across stakeholders, while a "9" indicated consistently positive outcomes. Two members of the research team rated each case, and any differences were discussed and resolved.[4]

## PRIMARY FINDINGS

Findings emerging from this study reveal a number of insights not only about the participants of the study and their work arrangements, but also

---

[3] Questionnaires were not sent to direct reports in three cases where the reduced load had recently ended, and the addresses of all subordinates were no longer known, and in one case due to administrative error of the interviewer.

[4] Members of the team developed the qualitative measure of success together, and received extensive training to ensure consistent use of the measure.

more generally about the relation between the amount of time spent at work and a number of personal and organizational outcomes.

## High Levels of Success from Multiple Perspectives

On average, the cases examined in this study were considered highly successful from the perspective of multiple stakeholders. The majority of cases (62 per cent) were in the High Success category (ratings of 7–9 on the scale described above), 31 per cent were in the Moderate Success group (ratings of 5 or 6), and 7 per cent received a Low Success rating.[5] There was no significant difference in the overall success ratings of managers' and professionals' reduced-load arrangements.[6] It should be noted that this sample was not randomly selected, and is not necessarily representative of all part-time professional and managerial employees. Nevertheless, the high success rate is significant in a variety of ways: first, it highlights the possibility of high levels of success of reduced-load work arrangements, among both professionals and managers, across a wide range of types of jobs, firms, and industries. Secondly, the consistency of evaluations across stakeholders suggests that the benefits to working less are generally not gained at others' expense. Thirdly, the data enable a closer examination of critical components of successful cases.

Additional indicators of success include:

- Managers and professionals gained an average of 18 hours per week by working reduced load
- Direct reports' ratings of their part-time managers' overall effectiveness averaged 7.2 out of 9 (with 1 indicating "very ineffective" and 9 indicating "very effective")
- Senior managers reported that target's individual work performance was generally maintained or improved
- Senior managers reported no significant negative impact on work unit performance
- 91 per cent of participants reported being happier and more satisfied with work–home balance
- 90 per cent of participants reported positive effects on their children: better relationships and more time with them

---

[5] The measure of success was not significantly correlated with tenure in the reduced-load work arrangement.

[6] While the global success rating was not significantly different between managers and professionals, other indicators suggested that managers were somewhat more successful on certain dimensions of reduced-load arrangements. For example, 43.5 per cent of the managers received promotions while on reduced load, compared with 21.6 per cent of the professionals.

Many of the comments regarding the success of these arrangements focused on an overall feeling of greater balance and increased capability of integrating different parts of their lives. One manager commented:

> Before it used to feel like I worked five days a week and I had a two-day weekend. Now it feels like I have a life . . . I have an integrated life that all works. And I work here, I work there, I play here, I play there, and it is just a patchwork quilt that all fits together and makes sense.

And another manager said:

> It suits exactly what I need, personally, in terms of balance in my life. So that I just don't think I, at this point, could work full-time because I value too much that time with my kids. And on the other hand I think if I were at home with the kids full-time, I would be looking for other outlets. And so this gives me such an ideal balance of adult, professional time, three days a week. And then I have my wonderful kids four days a week. And I get to earn money. And so it is just perfect.

When asked about the benefits of being on reduced load, one of the professionals said:

> In a nutshell, it gives me balance. It allows me to maintain my calm. It allows me to have a bit of everything. It allows me to be there more with my kids and do more things with them. And it allows me . . . you see, I don't think I'd be a good stay-at-home mom, full time. I think I'd find that a little tedious . . . because frankly, I think it is harder to stay at home and raise kids than to go to work. It is more challenging. And so this is kind of my stuff, my work. So it is kind of time for me, the work, to make a difference and add value that way. So I gain fulfillment from that and I think it allows me to be a better parent.

### Career Advancement Slowed, not Stopped

One of the most commonly voiced concerns about working reduced load was the potential negative impact upon career development. Some respondents worried that they would be perceived as less committed to the job by working part-time. While most, but not all, respondents believed they had made some career tradeoffs, about 2/3 believed that their career progress had not been stopped. Furthermore, about 35 per cent of the managers and professionals in the sample had received promotions while on reduced load. For another 33 per cent of the sample, their bosses reported that the company was still investing in these individuals and expected them to advance in their careers.

Independent of perceived or actual career advancement while on reduced load, many of the part-time professionals and managers talked about a personal redefinition of career success, and expressed a level of comfort with their choices and tradeoffs. For example, one professional said, "My focus has changed. Work is not the be-all, end-all anymore . . . . My priorities have shifted, and home is a lot more important, and this . . . allows me . . . to put focus where it needs to be." Another one said, "I feel like I have made some personal gains and sacrifices, and I've made peace with the way I'm juggling things." One of the professional participants commented:

> To me success has changed over the course of my career. But I would say at this point in my life, it is achieving a certain amount of financial stability, remuneration, whatever, and achieving a sense of contribution and satisfaction in what I do. So that says I couldn't make a lot of money and not enjoy what I was doing. Like, I would have to have both. But the success piece of it, I don't need the prestige and power, I just, I am quite able to contribute, lead, make a difference on a team environment. So I mean I have not desired to be president of [company name].

Another professional said:

> My time, as for all of us, is so valuable right now. I have a reasonable understanding of my capabilities and what I am able to contribute. And I seem to be pointed in the right direction. But I am not prepared to work my brains out anymore, if nobody else cares. Because I have got other places to put it. Wherein the past I was able to do that, for different reasons. It was just out of sheer energy and naivete. I would just work my little brains out, when it really didn't matter.

Finally, another commented:

> Career success? It has got to do with making a contribution to the organization that I am in and the company at large, really having an impact, feeling that something I'm doing isn't just pushing a pencil but that there are things that I can see and touch and feel that I know that I contributed towards making them what they are. And then there is a personal element of it, too, which is that I do it in a way that is really very honorable. That I keep my word, that I am a person of commitment that I fulfill my commitments, that I treat people well, fairly. That's it: that I do the job and that I do it in that particular way.

These case studies of career success while working part-time raise questions about what might be possible in career paths: they challenge traditional assumptions, supported by many organizational cultures, that working long hours and sacrificing personal time are accepted and expected parts of achieving success and advancement, and necessary elements for organizations to be competitive in the modern business world.

## Reduced-load Work not a Short-term Phenomenon

While some targets might have initiated their reduced-load arrangement as a temporary situation, for many of them it has become a new way of working and living, such that they no longer see it as short-term. The targets in this sample had been on reduced load for an average of 4.4 years. Furthermore, only 10 per cent are planning on returning to full time in the next three years.

## Success Hinges on Multiple Ingredients

Most respondents felt that many factors contributed to the success of these reduced-load work arrangements, rather than any single reason operating alone. All stakeholders concurred that success was multiply determined, citing reasons related to individual target characteristics and behavioral strategies, work-group factors, and organizational features. Eight of the top 12 factors cited are related to the individual working reduced load, suggesting that the workers themselves were perceived as largely responsible for making the negotiated work arrangement successful. The single most frequently cited facilitating factor was a supportive boss. Respondents believed that a boss's support was crucial for the approval and ongoing success of customized work arrangements.

The top 12 reported factors contributing to the success of the reduced-load arrangement included:

(1) *Individual characteristics and behavioral strategies*
- Concentrated, highly focused work style
- Strong performance record
- Unique skill set in high demand
- Flexibility
- High level of hard work and commitment
- Entrepreneurial style of taking initiative
- Strong, clear personal values around work, family and balance
- Ability to manage seamless communications, regardless of work schedule

(2) *Work-group factors*
- Supportive boss
- Competent and supportive peers and subordinates

(3) *Organizational characteristics*
- Organizational culture of employee-centered values
- Widely publicized work–life policies or programs

## Changes in the Use of Time at Work and at Home

By changing from full-time to part-time status, these professionals and managers gained an average of 18 hours per week for personal time, reducing their work hours from a mean of 50 hours per week before, to a mean of 32 hours in the part-time arrangement. In some cases, the job itself was redesigned by reducing the amount of work or the level of responsibility, but in other cases the participants continued to fulfill their same responsibilities on a part-time basis. The change to part-time status often meant a more intense *awareness* of how time is used, an actual change in how time at work is used, and a heightened sense of making every moment count. The reduced-load employees and other respondents reported that these workers had a very high level of focus and concentration when at work, an ability to identify priorities clearly and to work efficiently. They often skipped activities they perceived to be nonessential, reducing time spent socializing, celebrating the ends of projects, etc. (consistent with findings by Clark 1998). Some respondents mentioned that a significant tradeoff in skipping meetings, lunches, or social events in order to attain greater work efficiency was a subsequent reduction in networking opportunities and access to social information that can be instrumental in professional development. Many respondents mentioned that they made a point to schedule personal errands or doctors' appointments on their days off, thereby using their days in the office almost exclusively for work. These workers often displayed a high level of experimentation, creativity, and strategy about delegating work, when or when not to draw boundaries, communication with a boss about workload and opportunities, and communicating effectively and efficiently.

The extra time gained was spent in a variety of ways. It was often spent with children and other family members, getting chores and household work done, in community work (e.g. volunteering in schools), or on one's self (exercise or hobbies). There were more interactions with a variety of family stakeholders (teachers, neighbors, piano teachers, children's friends' parents, etc.), which often resulted in both increased demands and increased satisfaction from involvement. Many participants reported occasionally working from home on days off, by checking e-mail, taking phone calls, or going in to the office for certain meetings. However, they generally reported strong efforts to keep these contacts at a minimum. The extent to which respondents were able to draw clear boundaries between work and non-work time, or the extent to which they were comfortable with these boundaries, often seemed related to the overall success of the work arrangement.

## Organizational Outcomes

From the perspective of the work groups in organizations, direct reports were quite satisfied with the performance and supervision of their managers who were on reduced load. About half of the co-workers of part-time professionals and managers were rated as highly supportive of the arrangement. Another 25 per cent of the co-workers were not supportive, with some reporting that work not covered by the target ended up as an added responsibility for them.

From an organizational perspective, respondents in all stakeholder groups perceived a greater number of positive than negative outcomes from reduced-load work arrangements. Reported benefits included improved recruitment and retention efforts and a variety of advantages to managers (efficiency and productivity gains, staffing flexibility, etc.). The reduced-load work arrangements also enhance corporate image, and increase loyalty and motivation among employees. Interestingly, in some firms, even full-time co-workers expressed pride in working for a company that displayed an appreciation of the work–family conflicts faced by its workers and offered alternative work arrangements. In some cases, the targets' part-time arrangements also provided an opportunity for organizational learning. One executive reported that his company was re-examining its staffing policies in anticipation of a changing workforce, with increasing diversity in types of jobs, family situations, and financial and lifestyle needs. He said that his company was learning about the workplace and workforce of future generations of men and women, single and married, through the process of negotiating part-time work arrangements among today's mostly female professionals who are working to balance work and family concerns (see Lee, MacDermid & Buck 1999). Along with potential benefits of part-time work, organizations also reported concerns, including: how to manage the hassles and logistics for managers (scheduling complications, task allocation, or performance evaluations); how to manage the perceived inconsistency with workaholic cultures; how to avoid one case becoming a precedent and the resulting complexity that might ensue if more employees want to work part-time; and how to avoid the loss of talent in a highly competitive business environment.

## IMPLICATIONS FOR PERSONAL AND ORGANIZATIONAL LIFE

The relative success of these cases of reduced-load work by professionals and managers, coupled with the increasing proclivity of workers to experiment with other forms of alternative work arrangements, has a variety of implications for the theory and practice of organizational behavior. Examining changes in the way that people distribute their time between work and non-work life raises questions and offers insight into: (a) practices of effectively managing a workforce and the employment relationship; (b) workers' *experience* of time; and (c) the relation between personal identity and how time is spent.

## Management Practices: Time is Money

Workers' increasing pursuit of alternative work arrangements sheds new light on the phrase "time is money". Management has traditionally operated with a Newtonian perspective of linear time as a scarce resource, speaking of the currency of time and about "spending" time (Adam 1990, 1993; Daly 1996; Provonost 1986) When workers are "on the clock", their time is seen as not their own, but as belonging to the organization. With reduced-load work arrangements, in which individuals are voluntarily working fewer hours and being compensated less as well, workers are essentially "buying time". They are exchanging compensation for extra available time each week, but for many of the individuals in our sample, they were buying more than a certain number of hours. Many respondents suggested that they were buying control over their time, and buying flexibility within their lives. Indeed, for some targets in the sample, they were not actually reducing the amount of work, but essentially compressing a full-time workload into a part-time schedule, yet still being paid less. Most of these did not feel cheated, but instead felt that they were buying the right to adjust the scheduling of work to be more convenient with other priorities in their life, to increase the degrees of freedom in orchestrating the interplay of work, personal, and family life elements, or to set one's own boundaries rather than conform to expected norms of hours spent at work or a traditional meaning of success.

Organizations are faced with interesting challenges as more of their employees are willing to trade compensation for time and for perceived control and flexibility. Traditional financial sources of compensation may increasingly become less attractive to some workers, who place a higher priority upon a different way of living, and upon their feelings of balance and integration. As a result, organizations may increasingly be faced with requests for customized work arrangements and compensation packages, and, more generally, with more idiosyncratic employment relations, as they work to retain top talent in a competitive labor market.

The results of the current study, and work on part-time professionals by Clark (1998), provide examples of idiosyncratic negotiations for alternative work arrangements. In both studies, while there were sometimes official organizational policies in place regarding alternative work arrangements, many of the part-time arrangements were designed and implemented through idiosyncratic, personalized, and creative negotiations between the target individuals and those with whom they work, usually their boss. This tendency raises future challenges for the organizations involved, including, for whom will these arrangements be made available? And under what conditions? The research of Clark and that reported in this chapter suggest that highly valued employees, with unique skill sets, experience, and subsequent market power, as well as those who have been with the company long enough to be loyal and trusted, may have significant negotiating leverage in pursuing and sustaining non-traditional career paths. Looking to the future, as companies work to attract and retain valued employees, they may face challenges in having sufficient flexibility to offer customized packages, while maintaining meaningful guidelines that create acceptable criteria for equity. One senior manager made the following observation:

> My concern is very clear to everybody, that [s/he] is a superior employee, so nobody messes with it. If [s/he] was a more average employee, I think I'd get more heat on it. Another thing is, I really don't want to deal with it, but I don't really want anybody to come in here and ask for that. Some people, I'll just tell them "no". I'm not sure, I think we're on a little bit flaky ground there to say, "You are good, you can work at home," or "You're bad, you have to be watched." I think that's an area that gets a little messy.

In addition to the issues related to the unique motivations of employees, the emergence of alternative work arrangements in organizations also generates challenges to the traditional notion of "face time" as an indicator of commitment and success. Whether it is professionals working three days a week, telecommuters working from home offices, or virtual teams linked electronically from different locations, managers are less likely to actually see their direct reports working. In the cases of reduced-load work, many respondents commented that a factor that facilitated success in these arrangements was having a job in which there were objective measures to judge success, based on results/outcomes, not inputs, like the time present in the office. The shift from a production-focus to more results-oriented corporate cultures and a knowledge economy, coupled with an increasing number of workers who are not physically present for a "full-time" load, are concurrent factors increasing the pressure to find new ways of evaluating performance, and new ways of building, maintaining, and measuring trust.

Another effect of reduced-load work arrangements, as previously mentioned, is the opportunity it provides companies for organizational learning and adaptation. Many of the reduced-load workers in this study spoke about doing significant soul-searching to find new meanings of success and new means of professional development. Organizations will need to do similar exploration to find ways of accommodating the needs of these workers for purposes of recruitment and retention of valuable employees in a tight labor market, as well as an ongoing search for increased innovation and productivity. Recent studies of the way organizations approach the relationship between work life and personal life suggest that companies vary in the extent to which they see alternative work arrangements as something to be managed and contained, or as an opportunity for growth and learning (Friedman, Christensen & DeGroot 1998; Lee, MacDermid & Buck 1999). Future research can further examine the practices required to use isolated cases as pathways to innovation.

The increasing number of alternative work arrangements is just one of a number of indicators that the way in which time is distributed between work life and non-work life is a bottom-line business issue. A recent Health Canada report states that Canadian companies lose Can$2.7 billion annually because of employee absences, sickness, and stress from work–family conflict, and it costs the health care system an additional Can$45 million for related costs (Nebenzahl 1999). More companies are recognizing the business costs of long hours, heavy workloads, and feelings of work–family imbalances. Hewlett-Packard is taking out-of-the-ordinary steps to combat this issue, asking employees "to set annual goals not only for productivity but for leisure as well. They are expected to meet both, and if they fall short, their supervisors have to answer for it" (Kaufman 1999).

## Quantity of Time vs. the Experience of Time

The study of professionals and managers in reduced-load work arrangements gave numerous accounts of the power and impact of choice, control, and flexibility in the use of time. A resounding theme suggested that one of the major benefits of these work arrangements was not only the average 18 extra hours gained each week by reducing their work hours from about 50 to 32 hours, but also what those hours represented in terms of freedom and flexibility to use time creatively to fit professional, personal, and family needs. Rather than feeling overwhelmed with a seemingly impossible schedule of work and home activities, and a relatively rigid, inflexible structure, target individuals reported that their extra time away from work led to an overall feeling of more time and more opportunity to integrate different priorities. Furthermore, the feeling of *choice* about what to do with the extra time led to less stress and greater satisfaction. Whether the extra time was spent with children, doing household chores and cleaning, pursuing personal hobbies, or even doing work at home in order to feel caught up or to stay on top of pressing issues, the ability to choose that activity often seemed more significant than the inherent enjoyment of the activity itself in leading to greater overall satisfaction.

Some case studies in the present study suggest that more time at work is not necessarily always linked with better results, thereby challenging some traditional assumptions about time in organizations. Several managers reportedly performed better on reduced load. Their bosses attributed this to their being more fulfilled and balanced, more integrated, which allowed them to bring more energy, commitment, and creativity to their jobs. This greater fulfillment further fueled their motivation to make their arrangements work, thus continuing a cycle of excellent performance.

Many individuals' experiences in reduced-load work arrangements challenge traditional notions of Newtonian time in management and organizations. People tend to think of time as linear, as finite, as a scarce resource, and as a commodity (Adam 1990, 1993: Daly 1996; Provonost 1986). For example, time spent with the family or in leisure is seen as less time to sell or to earn money or to be productive (Smith 1999). However, many respondents spoke of a more elastic notion of time, in which the availability of more non-work time, and the ability to choose how to spend that time, created an expanded sense of time and new types of experiences of time. Some spoke of having more flexibility of time as an almost sacred time.

Most discussions of work–family conflict still imply a traditional notion of finite time: a gain in family time is a loss in the domain of work, and vice versa. It has been perceived as a zero sum game in most scenarios (Friedman, Christensen & DeGroot 1998). Even many discussions of "family-friendly" policies being cost-effective carry an implicit message that the domains of work and family are separate. The cost of these policies is viewed as a tradeoff, such that the cost becomes worthwhile when it significantly reduces other costs, operating as a process of cost containment. Instead, the cost of family-friendly policies could be viewed as an investment with significant growth potential, generating synergy. The experiences of some individuals working reduced load support this synergistic sort of view, such that their reduced-load arrangement contributes to a nourishing sense of expanded time, generating new possibilities and increased creativity, vitality, and resources.

Indeed, a recent report from the Norwegian firm Norsk Hydro (Fishman 1999) uses an agricultural analogy to explain the company's belief that balance can be a source of competitive advantage. One of the company's top executives suggests that "experienced farmers don't plant, harvest, plow, and reseed their fields season after season; they let the soil rest. Yet modern companies think nothing of working their most talented engineers, programmers, and managers ceaselessly." (Fishman 1999, p. 166). One way to avoid complete burnout is to spend time doing different things, rotating among different life domains, as a farmer might rotate among fields in order to best cultivate the land:

A rich life is a collection of compelling experiences, some of which involve work. Work that is all-consuming is unhealthy—for the individual, for the organization, and for the community. Time spent away from work is restorative. More to the point: Time spent outside work fuels work itself (Fishman 1999, p. 170).

## The Relation between Time and Personal Identity

The amount of time spent in work and non-work life, and the experience of time, appear related to important issues of identity, and suggest new areas of research investigation. The cases of managers and professionals working reduced load underscore the notion that people work differently and use time differently, and are more likely to thrive when afforded the freedom to follow their own rhythm. As Willa Cather once noted, "There are some things you learn best in calm, and some in storm" (cited in Ban Breathnach 1995). Some workers performed best in conditions of highly focused, concentrated work, with a clear separation of work time and non-work time. Others noted that it is essential that they have "downtime", or undistracted personal time, built into their schedule, which may lead to critical moments of inspiration and creativity, but in unpredictable ways. And among those who thrive on "downtime", some do it at work and on their personal time, and others do it in one domain and not the other. Research could further investigate the impact of personal rhythms of time use upon personal well-being, creativity, and performance.

The reduced-load work cases also showed ways in which individuals' work status was linked with their self-perception and well-being. The designation of "full-time" and "part-time", for both work and family domains, had powerful connotations and meaning for many workers. For some individuals, moving to part-time work led to a more fulfilled identity, as if being a part-time professional and a part-time parent added up to a more complete identity, compared with a more fragmented image of a full-time worker, feeling absent and dissociated from home life, and the corresponding identities of parent and spouse. They were happy and felt more *themselves*, as if the change in time allocation allowed them to express themselves more authentically. One individual commented:

> Sometimes I look at other people's lives and I think, "Well, do I want to do this? Do I want to work full time and have the big job and sort of the career things, too?" I think, "No way." Even though on my days off I'm doing the grocery shopping on Thursdays and doing the carpool, I like doing that. I'm the kind of person who likes to do lots of different things. And I find that very energizing, rather than doing only one thing.

For other participants, however, it was clear that their intention to feel more balanced and integrated was not fulfilled by moving to a reduced-load arrangement, and instead generated more stress and discontent.

Some individuals reported that by working part-time, they no longer felt "full-time anything". They were tormented by not being fully available for their colleagues *or* their family. One professional from the present study commented:

> I think that if I worked full-time, I would do better and be happier at the job. It is very difficult to do something half way. I think it is almost analogous to when I was in college, I was mostly an "A" or "B" student. And one time I took a Pass/Fail course. And in this . . . course, I just listened to the lectures and didn't do any work outside of the class. And I managed to pass the class. But I never felt like I had a very good understanding of what was going on, and I found it tremendously frustrating. I mean, to the point where I said to myself at the time, "I cannot imagine anybody going through life as a 'C' student, only marginally getting by." So I see that as analogous.

Numerous comments highlighted the sense in which "full-time" and "part-time" can carry powerful meanings and emotional associations. For some, working full-time carried a notion of professionalism, pride, commitment, and accomplishment. For others, the "full-time" label was a continual and even painful reminder of other parts of their life that were not receiving full-time, or even partial, attention. Many workers found that by changing the number of hours they worked, they subsequently were able to change their lifestyles and perhaps even their identities. Others might attempt that personal transformation by changing the number of hours worked, yet find that they still need to confront deeper or additional issues about their choices, their marriage, their job, their household work distribution, etc.

For many professionals, definitions of success and identity are interlinked, in the sense that they evaluate themselves and base their identities upon their accomplishments. And based upon traditional norms, to be successful at something means to give full commitment and 100 per cent effort to it. So many workers, especially women, are feeling torn by the desire to be successful in all areas of their life, but unable to give full time and commitment to each of those domains. Furthermore, they are often feeling that they no longer "fit" in a work arrangement that requires a full-time job design and expectations of full commitment. McKenna (1997) writes that

> . . . it had simply become too exhausting emotionally and psychologically to keep working on terms that were increasingly not my own. I felt tremendous sadness as I saw that my most enduring relationship—that of my career and me—had changed and was possibly ending. It would have been a critical mistake to conclude that motherhood was the cause or the solution of the problem. Motherhood was completely beside the point. All it did,

really, was focus the problem—that I was working in an environment that wasn't designed for a woman like me (p. 9).

She continues to say that each woman who is pursuing some sort of non-traditional career path is making a

> magical shift from being identified by her work to being just "who she was". . . . The issue here is the conflict itself, the tear between a life built around who we thought we should be as career women and who we have become in the process of our lives (p. 15).

Finally, another aspect of the relationship between time use and personal identity comes from a different angle: rather than considering the impact of how individuals spend their time upon how they think and feel about themselves, some respondents referred to the impact of self-awareness upon how they allocate their time. Respondents mentioned, sometimes explicitly and sometimes implicitly, that clear self-knowledge about what they valued, how they ranked their values, and what trade-offs they were comfortable making, enabling them to choose and pursue alternative work arrangements, or other methods of finding balance in their lives. One professional captured this idea when talking about what advice she would give to others who wanted to find more balance between work and family:

> What advice would I have? To tell yourself the truth about what you want and what is important to you. And to know yourself. And know what enables you to be a whole, balanced person. You know, some people . . . are that way by working full time, or by being stay-at-home moms full time. So, because what works best for me doesn't necessarily mean it is best for everybody. And you know, I recognize that . . . . So, know what is right for you . . . . And then I think, not to apologize for what you choose. You know, make the choices. See, I make choices and I know there are some tradeoffs with those choices. You know, so I'm not going to feel badly about—I'm not going to sit here and lament the fact that I'm not a director in the organization. I don't want that responsibility right now. Maybe I'll never want it.

For some, the ability to articulate a clear sense of what mattered to them seemed linked with a clear motivation to live in a way that was more aligned with those priorities. One possible way to accomplish this was to pursue a reduced-load work arrangement, thereby altering the distribution of work and non-work time in their lives.

In summary, for many workers today, their efforts to creatively redesign their work experience seems linked with larger desires and yearnings for self-expression. More individuals speak of having a life that "works", or just of "having a life", suggesting that "a life" includes

Levy, E. S., Flynn, P. M. & Kellogg, D. M. (1997) Customized work arrangements in the accounting profession: an uncertain future. Technical report to the Alfred P. Sloan Foundation.

McKenna, E. P. (1997) *When Work Doesn't Work Anymore: Women, Work, and Identity*. New York: Dell Publishing.

Meiksins, P. & Whalley, P. (1995) Technical working and reduced work. Paper presented at the Annual Meeting of the American Sociological Association, Washington, D.C.

Mirchandani, K. (1998) No longer a struggle: teleworkers' reconstruction of the work–non-work boundary. In P. J. Jackson & J. M. Vander Wielen (Eds), *Teleworking: International Perspectives* (pp. 118–135). London: Routledge.

Moen, P. (1999) *The Cornell Couples and Career Study*. Ithaca, NY: Cornell University.

*Montreal Gazette* (1999) Stressed out at work. **15 November**: B2.

Nebenzahl, D. (1999) Family and work—conflict growing. *Montreal Gazette*, **14 June**: C1, C6.

Provonost, G. (1986) Introduction: time in a sociological and historical perspective. *International Social Science Journal*, **38**: 5–18.

Scandura, T. A. & Lankau, M. J. (1997) Relationships of gender, family responsibility and flexible work hours to organizational commitment and job satisfaction. *Journal of Organizational Behavior*, **18**(4): 377–391.

Schor, J. (1991) *The Overworked American*. New York: Basic Books.

Seron, C. & Ferris, K. (1995) Negotiating professionalism: the gendered social capital of flexible time. *Work and Occupations*, **22**: 22–47.

Smith, S. C. (1999) Specialization paper. Unpublished manuscript, Purdue University.

Tobin, A. M. (1999) No time left for family, friends. *Montreal Gazette*, **10 November**: 1–2.

CHAPTER 3

# All in the Timing: Team Pacing Behaviors in Dynamic Conditions

Mary J. Waller
*Department of Business Administration, University of Illinois at Urbana–Champaign, USA*

## INTRODUCTION

The business environment faced by organizations today can change at an incredibly fast pace. For example, the NATO bombing of the Chinese Embassy in Yugoslavia unexpectedly and instantaneously added to the pressures faced by US businesses located in China. Other firms face new threats from Europe's freshly welded economy and from Internet-based competitors that seem to steal market share overnight. Organizations unable to match the pace of change whirling about them are quickly swallowed or destroyed by their more nimble counterparts.

Facing such a hypercompetitive landscape, many organizations now rely on teams, rather than individuals, to analyze quickly, and respond to, critical problems and situations. Additionally, the downsizing of the 1980s and early 1990s led to the reduction of middle management layers and the formation of more self-managed teams at or below that hierarchical level in organizations. Thus, not only are organizations using teams to respond accurately and quickly to problems, there are more teams available in organizations to deploy. Given the increased reliance on teams and the increased pace with which teams must act, this chapter focuses on how teams are able to solve problems and make decisions—often juggling multiple, complex tasks—under time-pressured situations.

*Trends in Organizational Behavior*, Volume 7. Edited by C. L. Cooper and D. M. Rousseau.
Copyright © 2000 John Wiley & Sons, Ltd.

The research literature on group and team behavior has begun to focus on the importance of the timing of team responses and behaviors. Recent work has been published, for example, on how groups pace their task performance under strict deadlines (Gersick 1988, 1989), on teams' reactions in "high velocity" environments (Eisenhardt 1989), and on the timing of team behaviors during critical non-routine events (Waller 1999). This chapter offers an overview of two new areas of research concerning how teams pace their work under deadline situations. One particularly promising area of research concerns team polychronicity—or the simultaneous performance of more than one task by a team. Given the rate at which tasks are presented to teams by their dynamic environments, and considering the implications of teams not finishing tasks by assigned deadlines, the ability of teams to perform multiple tasks simultaneously seems quite important. The second area of research focuses on the ability of teams to complete tasks under shifting deadline conditions. Much previous research on team performance has focused on teams working under stable deadline conditions; however, in real organizations, teams often face deadlines that unexpectedly move forward or backward due to competitors' actions, client demands, or changes in organizational strategy. Taken together, both areas of research offer the potential for new insights regarding the management of teams in dynamic environments.

## POLYCHRONICITY

Polychronicity is the simultaneous performance of multiple tasks. A time-pressured executive may, for example, simultaneously check e-mail, discuss a sales report on the speakerphone, and sign outgoing letters. Similarly, a time-pressured software development team of five people may use two team members to write project specifications, two team members to schedule human and computer resources, and one member to interface with the client, with all team members working on their respective tasks simultaneously. Earlier research on polychronicity focused on the ability or propensity of individuals to engage in multiple tasks simultaneously (Bluedorn, Kaufman & Lane 1992), but more recent work has explored actual polychronic behavior in teams (Waller, Giambatista & Zellmer-Bruhn 1999), in organizations (Benabou 1999) and even across national cultures (Cotte & Ratneshwar 1999). The Waller, Giambatista & Zellmer-Bruhn (1999) work is particularly relevant for discussion here, since it focused on how individual team members' attention to time affects how teams work under deadline situations. Waller, Giambatista & Zellmer-Bruhn (1999) studied teams of three and four members working on a creative task under deadline conditions. The researchers wanted to understand how an individual team member's time-urgent behavior might affect the team's polychronic behavior. Individuals who are time urgent tend to be more attentive to time and deadlines than other individuals (Strube, Deichmann & Kickham 1989). Little is known, however, about the effects such individuals may have on team outcomes. For example, if a team working under a deadline has one member who emerges as a time-urgent "clock-watcher" as compared with the rest of the team, does his or her presence increase or decrease the ability of the team to perform multiple tasks simultaneously? Because previous research indicates that the amount of polychronic behavior may be linked to performance (Slocombe & Bluedorn 1999), this question had particular relevance.

The researchers gave each of 26 three- or four-person groups a deadline (average 60 min) to complete a creative task. The task involved the teams creating a 60 s radio commercial for a major airline. The teams were given written information about the airline, guidelines for the commercial (for example, the commercial had to stress low cost), an assortment of music and sound effect compact discs, a compact disc player, and a budget that limited the number of actors, sound effects, and music tracks that could be used in the commercial. During their development of the commercial, each team was videotaped. The videotapes were later analyzed to determine the amount of time-related behavior of each individual (i.e. looking at the clock or watch, mentioning the amount of time remaining), and the amount of polychronic behavior of the team.

The researchers found that having a time-urgent individual on the team increased monotonic (versus polychronic) behavior in the team. In other words, having a "clock-watcher" on the team tended to bring the team together to focus on one primary task at a time. This result has implications for managers of teams in that, if polychronic behavior is necessary in order for the team to finish its job on time, then managers may not wish to include highly time-urgent individuals on some teams. These research results echo work on time management principles that likewise suggests teams may have "time taskmasters", or those individuals in teams who are most likely to be deadline-driven (Douglass & Douglass 1992). Other work on time management behavior suggests that individuals likely to be time urgent or polychronic also were more likely than others to (1) believe that they perform best under pressure and (2) strive to complete tasks on time (Kaufman-Scarborough & Lindquist 1999). More research should be completed concerning the influence of such time-urgent individuals (for instance, research using different types of tasks and different deadlines), for the ultimate implications may be extremely useful for managers of teams that work under time pressure.

## SHIFTING DEADLINES

While issues of polychronicity are important to understand, like most published research on teams, neither the research on team polychronicity nor the research cited earlier concerning team pacing has specifically investigated how teams adjust their pacing when deadlines change. Given the dynamic environments surrounding them, teams often face shifting deadlines—that is, deadlines that are unexpectedly made either shorter or longer. For example, while developing a new version of the Taurus, Ford contracted the seat design tasks to the Lear Corporation (Walton 1997). Unfortunately for the Lear design team, by the time Ford finally approved the contract, most other engineering work on the car had been underway for a year. This created an enormous sense of time pressure for the Lear team, which also desperately needed technical help. The first versions of seats from Lear could not be assembled without breaking off several plastic pieces, and seat fabric ripped at the seams, pushing prototype and production schedules back. Ford responded by attacking Lear and shifting deadlines for the Lear team forward. As the Ford program manager stated, "(F)or whatever reason, you've got to keep the pressure on; people slack off. And Lear's slacking off."

Situations like Lear's occur often in organizations, and these situations illuminate two important research questions. First, how do teams pace themselves when their deadlines suddenly change? Secondly, do some pacing behaviors seem to work better than others? An ongoing research project by Waller, Giambatista & Zellmer-Bruhn focuses on these questions. Using the same radio commercial task described previously, the researchers initially told each of the 26 teams that they would have 60 min to complete the task. Then, after 10 min had elapsed, the researchers interrupted nine of the groups and told them that because of the client's travel plans, they now only had 50 min total to complete the task. Conversely, the research interrupted nine other teams and told them that because of the client's travel plans, they now had 70 min total to complete the task. The remaining eight teams were not interrupted and served as a control group.

When the performance of the teams was compared across conditions, the researchers found that teams whose deadlines were shifted either back to 50 min or forward to 70 min outperformed the teams whose deadlines were not changed. The researchers were surprised to find no significant difference in performance between the 50 min and 70 min deadline teams. Initially, researchers expected that the 70 min teams would outperform all other teams, given the complexity of the task. What pacing behaviors allowed the 50 min teams to perform as well as teams given 70 min, and why did teams with shifted deadlines outperform uninterrupted teams?

To answer the first question, researchers returned to the patterns of behaviors exhibited by the teams over time. Using new information from the polychronicity research described earlier, they coded the occurrences of polychronic behavior across time for each team. The 50 min groups used significantly more polychronic behavior over time than did the 70 min groups. Because they split into subgroups and performed multiple tasks simultaneously, they were able to match the performance of teams that had significantly more time resources. This finding underscores the importance of understanding how individuals and teams react to deadline pressure.

Regarding the reason that teams with shifted deadlines outperformed uninterrupted teams, the researchers found that after the announcements of deadline changes, the teams with shifted deadlines exhibited more attention to time, generated more ideas for the commercial, worked more on evaluating and choosing among alternative ideas, and generally had higher activity levels than did the teams with stable deadlines. Previous research found that attention to time acts as a catalyst for teams, motivating task-oriented action (Gersick 1989). The shifting deadline research described here found a similar effect in that heightened attention to time may have motivated some groups to engage in these higher levels of behavior.

What are the practical implications of this research? First, the research indicates that fundamental behavioral changes in pacing take place in teams when their deadlines change. These changes are accompanied by increased levels of overall activity and heightened awareness of time in teams. Managers should note that each time they or clients shift teams' deadlines, the team members expend the energy necessary to change pacing behavior. Managers in some situations may do well to attempt to insulate teams from numerous deadline shifts, and future research should investigate how many changes teams are able to respond to before they become de-sensitized to deadline shifts and are unable or unwilling to adapt to them. Conversely, given that the teams with stable deadlines were the lowest performers in this study, managers may wish to interrupt teams in stable situations with an artificially-shifted deadline or call attention to time for teams in some other way. To investigate whether a simple interruption might be sufficient, Waller, Giambatista & Zellmer-Bruhn compared the effects of simply interrupting teams after 10 min and interrupting them after 10 min with a shifted deadline announcement. Those teams that were simply interrupted performed no differently than did the teams in the stable (uninterrupted) deadline condition. This finding suggests that calling attention to time in some way is more likely to be beneficial for team performance as compared with simply interrupting teams with other information.

## CONCLUSIONS

Organizations are facing increasingly dynamic business environments. As a result, many teams are called upon in organizations to make critical decisions under extreme time pressure. The research described in this chapter helps clarify what we know about team performance in time-pressured situations. Team polychronicity research indicates that highly time-urgent individuals tend to focus the team on one task at a time, rather than encourage the team to perform multiple tasks simultaneously. Research on shifting deadlines suggests that groups working under very tight time constraints can use polychronic behavior to compensate for their lack of time resources. Taken together, these two findings suggest that future research should investigate whether having time-urgent individuals in groups with tight deadlines is associated with lower team performance. The results of this future research, used in conjunction with questionnaires already developed to measure individuals' polychronicity propensity, could be important tools for managers of teams working in dynamic, time-pressured conditions.

Future research should also investigate the effects of deadlines on other team outcomes. For example, as deadlines become shorter, the creativity of teams' responses may approach a more bimodal distribution—either very creative or very perfunctory—with some teams being able to achieve high levels of performance and others perceiving near-impossible conditions. Similarly, future research should attempt to identify the point at which deadlines become so restrictive as to de-motivate most teams by leading them to perceive the task before them as now impossible. Finally, future research should investigate the ability of teams working under shifting deadlines to muster the stamina needed to produce highly creative or accurate outcomes under a string of time-pressured situations.

As organizations struggle to keep pace with changing regulations, competitors, clients, and technology, they will most likely continue to rely on teams to make quick, accurate decisions. Through experience, organizations are becoming more aware that some teams seem able to "rise to the occasion" and consistently produce high-quality results under extreme time pressure, while other teams seem to fall apart under similar conditions. Research that investigates how teams perform tasks under time-starved situations, coupled with research that identifies the behaviors allowing teams to perform at peak levels under these conditions, should lead to the development of useful tools for managers and members of teams in a variety of fast-paced organizational settings.

# REFERENCES

Benabou, C. (1999) Polychronicity and temporal dimensions of work in learning organizations. *Journal of Managerial Psychology*, **14**: 257–268.

Bluedorn, A. C., Kaufman, C. F. & Lane, P. M. (1992) How many things do you like to do at once? An introduction to monochronic and polychronic time. *Academy of Management Executive*, **6**: 17–26.

Cotte, J. & Ratneshwar, S. (1999) Juggling and hopping: what does it mean to work polychronically? *Journal of Managerial Psychology*, **14**: 184–204.

Douglass, M. E. & Douglass, D. N. (1992) *Time Management for Teams*. New York: Amacom.

Eisenhardt, K. (1989) Making fast strategic decisions in high-velocity environments. *Academy of Management Journal*, **32**: 543–576.

Gersick, C. J. G. (1988) Time and transition in work teams: toward a new model of group development. *Academy of Management Journal*, **31**: 9–41.

Gersick, C. J. G. (1989) Marking time: predictable transition in task groups. *Academy of Management Journal*, **32**: 274–309.

Kaufman-Scarborough, C. & Lindquist, J. D. (1999) Time management and polychronicity: comparisons, contrasts, and insights for the workplace. *Journal of Managerial Psychology*, **14**: 288–312.

Slocombe, T. E. & Bluedorn, A. C. (1999) Organizational behavior implications of the congruence between preferred polychronicity and experienced work-unit polychronicity. *Journal of Organizational Behavior*, **20**: 75–99.

Strube, M. J., Deichmann, A. K. & Kickham, T. (1989) Time urgency and the Type A behavior pattern: time investment as a function of cue salience. *Journal of Research in Personality*, **23**: 287–301.

Waller, M. J. (1999) The timing of adaptive group responses to nonroutine events. *Academy of Management Journal*, **42**: 127–137.

Waller, M. J., Giambatista, R. C. & Zellmer-Bruhn, M. (1999) The effects of individual time urgency on group polychronicity. *Journal of Managerial Psychology*, **14**: 244–256.

Walton, M. (1997) *Car: A Drama of the American Workplace*. New York: Norton & Company.

CHAPTER 4

# Alternative Ways of Describing Time in Cross-cultural Careers Research

Cherlyn Skromme Granrose
*Campbell School of Business, Berry College, USA*

## INTRODUCTION

"Career barriers", "career jungle gyms", "career networks", "career crossroads", "career entrenchment", "career mainstream", "cyclic models of career motivation", "inner and outer circles of career elites", and "temporary careers" are career images present in recent Euro-American literature (Agbor-Baiyee 1997; Allmendinger *et al.* 1997; Earls 1998; Gunz, Jalland & Evans 1998; Hall 1997; Iberra 1997; London 1998). Describing careers as "middle class white men making a single linear motion through space and time in a single organization" no longer fits the way many people think about careers. Complex views of careers include beliefs and feelings as well as jobs; non-work as well as work aspects of life development; and entries and exits, starts and stops, and cycles of boundary-less careers across multiple organizations (Arthur & Rousseau 1996). Today the concept of careers extends even further to include careers in multiple cultural contexts. Global competition, electronic media and communications, organizational mergers, and immigration are bringing multicultural contexts into the most remote or impoverished locations (Zahra 1999). Thus, most careers of the twenty-first century will not occur in the context of a single cultural setting, even if individuals do not move from their home town during their lifetime. The old assumptions that careers occur in one organization, in one culture, using one skill set, with

*Trends in Organizational Behavior*, Volume 7. Edited by C. L. Cooper and D. M. Rousseau.
Copyright © 2000 John Wiley & Sons, Ltd.

one goal of upward mobility, do not fit contemporary reality. There are some signs that the old methodologies also do not fit the new career complexity. The purpose of this chapter is to examine new ways to describe the content and the time dimension of these contemporary, complex, cross-cultural careers using linear images or pictures as a descriptive and analytic methodology.

Whether we talk about cultures of national groups, ethnic groups, or organizational groups, careers have different concepts in different cultures. In fact, the concept of a career may not be explicit in many cultures. But in most cultures there is a concept of work and there is a concept of time, and it is seeking new ways to describe how the meaning of time is attached to the concept of work that is the focus of this chapter. If we continue to hold a definition of a work career as work-related beliefs, values, and behaviors that extend across time, then we can no longer ignore the impact of different cultural conceptualizations of time on career research and practice.

## CULTURAL DIFFERENCES IN KEY DIMENSIONS OF CAREER TIME

Contemporary career concepts that extend across multiple cultures must consider several key dimensions of time. These attributes of time include:

- Time orientation
- Time extension
- Rhythm
- Pace
- Multiple processes of polychronicity, synchronicity, and entrainment

Considering the way each of these dimensions of time may vary across cultures and may affect career thinking will provide the vocabulary we need to discuss alternative ways to illustrate and analyze career concepts in a multicultural environment.

### Time Orientation

Different cultures place different emphasis on the past, the present, or the future (Kluckhohn & Strodtbeck 1961). Members of past-oriented cultures focus on tradition when they interpret events and when they decide what to do in the future. For example, understanding career mechanisms in a society with a rich traditional orientation toward the past might require learning more about precedents, such as the occupation of one's father or mother. In contrast, describing careers in future-oriented societies such as the United States may require a heavy emphasis on goals, aspirations, and future risks or consequences in order to capture important career dimensions. Those who live in present-oriented societies focus on short-term problem solving and present activities. Explaining a career as something that extends across the length of one life might have little meaning for inhabitants in these societies or organizations.

## Time Extension

Time extension is the duration, or time horizon that members of a culture use when thinking about careers, whether this duration extends into the past or into the future. American career counselors often ask participants how long into the future they are thinking when planning their careers and this is a specific measure of future time extension in individual thinking. Scholars who study differences in industry life cycles from the 30-year cycle of investment decisions in industrial materials firms to the monthly cycles of high tech computer software firms illustrate wide variations in organizational conceptions of time extension (Williams 1999).

Measuring time extension may be very complex when working in a culture that has a long time extension combined with extreme past or future orientation. For example, if we explore career beliefs in societies such as India or Thailand, where many people value reincarnation as a central religious tenet, we have to consider career beliefs that extend across more than one lifetime. In the United States, advocates of environmental protection urge organizations to think of the impact of their actions on future generations as well (Schettler et al. 1999). Although careers that extend across generations are not presently considered in the Euro-American career literature, cross-generation beliefs certainly confound practicing managers. These managers may attempt to use immediate career rewards to motivate employees but may be met with indifference by individuals who value external rewards or cross-generation rewards more highly. New methodologies that include the dimension of time extension are needed to fit these ways of thinking about contemporary careers.

## Rhythm

Rhythm is the pattern of pauses or disjunctions or recurrent events that occur in a process as it extends across time. Career rhythms might be used to characterize periods of employment and unemployment or periods of advancement and plateaux of individuals or groups of individuals in an organization. The addition of a market economy sector to the planned economy of China has resulted in a career rhythm for some people that is punctuated by movement between employers quite different from the former long-term government assignment to a work unit (Kelley & Luo 1999). Just as music from different cultures contains unique rhythmic patterns, there is no reason to expect that career rhythms in different cultures should be any less complex, but this possibility remains largely unexplored.

## Pace

Western management career literature is strewn with references to pace, with the usual assumption that faster is better. For example, managers may be on the fast track or the slow track to upward mobility. "On time", "saving time", "wasting time" or "spending time" in one or another career alternative also express the culture-specific and value-laden nature of many dimensions of career pace. Contemporary employees may worry about a pace of organizational change that is so rapid their skills become outdated. In their response they may rush to learn new skills to be able to keep up with rapidly changing organizational demands or they may choose to steer their careers toward occupations or organizations where the pace of change is more in keeping with their own internal pace.

But a rapid pace is not always valued. In Singapore or Hong Kong, job hopping, or the practice of shifting frequently from one firm to another in order to obtain a promotion or a raise when these economies were expanding rapidly, is considered quite bad form (Chow 1997).

## Multiple Processes: Polychronicity, Synchronicity and Entrainment

Multiple career processes that may occur during the same time period can be described by the terms polychronicity, synchronicity, and entrainment. To apply these concepts of time to careers we must identify the multiple career processes and the indicators of relevant phases or cycles (Hall, 1983).

### Polychronicity

This is the dimension of time that refers to more than one process occurring simultaneously. In US culture, one example of career polychronicity is when employment career and family career are considered simultaneously in thinking about an individual career. The advancement of more women into higher levels of organizations and into important human resource management positions has increased the salience of this aspect of career dynamics. Polychronicity might also occur when organizational career processes are compared with individual work–family career cycles (Gordon & Whelan 1998; Millikin, Martins & Morgan 1998). Other examples of polychronicity may occur in analyzing careers of individuals in different occupational groups in the same organizations, where a different career process may occur for each occupation, or in describing careers in different organizations or industries where different jungle gym career processes exist (Gunz, Jalland & Evans 1998). In each culture, the processes included in a polychronic view of careers and the definition of a cycle may vary.

*Synchronicity*

This refers to instances when multiple processes coincide in time. Synchronicity of career patterns might occur in a dual-career family employed by a multinational firm when both members desire relocation simultaneously. Career synchronicity may or may not occur in career patterns of different members of a cross-functional work team, or in the careers of those in the same organization on expatriate assignments compared with those in the home office (Dowling, Welch & Schuler 1999; Jassawalla & Sashittal 1999).

*Entrainment*

This is the phenomenon where one cyclic process becomes captured by, and set to oscillate in rhythm with, another process. Either speed or cycle phases may be synchronized in entrainment (McGrath & Kelly 1986). Dual-career couples who have managed to match the importance of employment and family in ways that are synergistic for each partner might be examples of career entrainment. Members of virtual teams or members of different units in modular organizations or different stakeholders of the same organization also might find that their separate career processes become entrained as individual people or units try to coordinate their functioning with others (Frooman 1999).

We do not have a systematic catalogue of the multiple processes included in careers in different cultures and we have few systematic ways of analyzing cyclic phenomena when multiple cycles are occurring in the same time frame. When we begin to look at careers across multiple organizations, even more complex patterns of career polychronicity, synchronicity, and entrainment (or the lack thereof) occur. Managers can use computer programs to tabulate the polychronicity of many individual employee careers in a given organization by identifying how many employees will be in each type of position in each location at different points of time. However, we lack common tools to create and measure the extent to which multiple career patterns exhibit synchronicity or entrainment.

In reviewing these dimensions of career time, it is clear that managers and scholars have explored some aspects of time extensively, such as career pace and career extension, whereas other dimensions, such as career time orientation and career entrainment remain relatively untouched. To some extent this is a reflection of ethnocentric perspectives that assume a single way of looking at careers and at time. But it is also due to the difficulty encountered because of the complexity of the task and lack of tools that might fit a cross-cultural career reality. The second part of this chapter explores tools that might be used to add to our understanding of different cultural concepts of career time.

## POSSIBLE WAYS OF MEASURING CAREER TIME ACROSS CULTURES

One way to meet the challenge of understanding career time in multiple cultural contexts is to explore alternative methods of describing and measuring career time. The traditional way of expanding research on a subject across cultures will be described first and then several possible alternatives suggested.

### Expanding Ethnographic Alternatives to Survey Techniques

Euro-American measures of career time have asked individuals to answer survey questions about their career history, their career timetables or planning horizons, or family and leisure dimensions of careers. A typical time-related question at the individual level might be "How far into the future do you have plans for your career?"

| 1 | 2 | 3 | 4 | 5 |
|---|---|---|---|---|
| Day by day | 1 year | 2–5 years | 6–10 years | More than 10 years |

At the organizational level some researchers might ask "How long do managers stay in the same position in this organization?" These data can be analyzed for various dimensions of extension, orientation, rhythm, and pace within and across individuals but when this exploration is conducted across different cultures, the very meanings of the terms also need to be explored. Questions such as these and detailed career histories first need to be placed in the cultural context, when the alternative meanings of such things as "The same position" (skills, title, rank, etc.) or "career plans" (general idea or specific strategy) can be explicated.

Traditional survey techniques have serious limitations for cross-cultural exploration. The cultural assumptions of the research scholar alter every stage of the research process, from formulation of the question, through selection of the cultures to include, choice of the measures, and interpretation of results. Practitioners who have tried to extend this method into cross-cultural contexts may use comparable sampling, translate and back translate the instruments into culturally appropriate language and use interview techniques designed to elicit cultural differences in the way people are thinking about careers (Granrose 1997). These studies are open to serious criticism, however, because they do not explore whether the meanings and units of measurement of time and work implied by the wording of the questions and the alternatives fit the new cultural context. To counter this criticism scholars suggest that we should (1) identify the cultural context of each concept, such as various dimensions of career time orientation; (2) develop culturally appropriate ways of measuring career time with instruments constructed in each culture; and (3) identify common elements that can be used to compare career time across cultures (Berry *et al.* 1992; Punnett & Shenkar 1996). It will be many years before we have culturally specific definitions and culturally specific measures of the career time constructs in many different cultures. Even when they are constructed there is little assurance that the ideas will overlap in measurably and practically meaningful ways. A more serious limitation is that most of the conceptualizations of time in these questions assume a linear, unidirectional view of time that may not be appropriate for all other cultures.

Another set of alternatives that increases the possibility that people may be able to express themselves in culturally consistent ways is to use lines, drawings, and maps in addition to language to explore the concept of career time. While these techniques do not avoid many of the problems inherent in cross-cultural questionnaire research they do open up some new possibilities.

## Career-line Drawing

The inspiration for the first of these techniques comes from an exercise that career guidance professionals sometimes use—drawing a career line. In this exercise, the participant usually is asked, "Please draw a line representing your life from the beginning to the end and label significant points." "Now could you explain what your line means to you?" By altering the traditional directions to encourage the drawing of multiple lines extending both into the past and into the future one can create measures of time extension and orientation that are not unilinear and unidirectional. Placement of events, bumps, curves, and other identifiable points can be measured for rhythm and pace. Directions to draw multiple lines for the important processes in other life domains could be used to identify polychronicity, synchronicity, and entrainment within individuals. Analysis of the measurements of lines from multiple people could be used to create databases for organizations if the units of measurement were selected for a specific purpose and for the appropriate meaning in the cultural backgrounds represented in the group.

This methodology does not circumvent the need to interpret results in light of the cultural context represented. It does reduce, but not eliminate, some of the problems inherent in the translation of pre-existing multi-item measures. Construct equivalence, item equivalence, and scale equivalence across multiple cultures are so difficult to achieve that many fail to conduct cross-cultural research and others ignore the problems and produce results impossible to interpret. The draw-a-line technique still needs to consider construct equivalence and perhaps some new meaning of the term "scale equivalence" will have to be determined. This method does begin to address the existing problem of measuring only unilinear, unidirectional views of time.

## Draw a Career Picture

A multidimensional technique derived both from the draw-a-line tradition of career counseling and from the draw-a-person therapeutic tradition is to ask respondents to draw a picture of their careers (McElhaney 1969; Alland 1983; Granrose 1995). Although considerable controversy surrounds this idea, some believe that pictorial perceptions and portrayal, like specific languages, make use of specific cultural codes (Gombrich 1977) and culturally determined skills (Serpell & Deregowski 1980) that might make this technique particularly appropriate for capturing cultural concepts of time.

One example can illustrate how this technique identifies different ways of thinking about career time in different cultures. In an ongoing study of the careers of Asian managers, we used pictures as a means of measurement of career concepts that might be less tied to linear, goal-oriented, particularistic, thinking of the United States and more reflective of indirect, non-verbal, cyclic, holistic communications (Althen 1988; Granrose 1997; Granrose & Huang 1999). Pre-tests conducted in Hong Kong used a variety of ways to ask participants to draw images related to work. Structured questions proved cumbersome and still linked to linear thinking, while structure-less blank paper approaches yielded equally blank looks from respondents. On the basis of several rounds of pre-tests the methodology was modified to provide some structure and some alternatives in asking participants to make a drawing representing their careers and to write a narrative explaining their drawing.

Thinking of a career as all of the jobs you have in your working life, extending across time, draw a picture to represent your career from its beginning to its end. For example, it may be a line that goes up or down or curves or spirals. It may be a mixture of words and pictures. There is no correct way to draw this picture, just express yourself in your own way. On your picture, label the point or piece that represents the present.

This was followed by about 4 inches of blank space and then the question was posed: "Looking at the picture you have drawn, how would you describe what it means to you? You can put labels on your picture to help you explain it." During the interview, additional information was elicited by asking the participants to describe their pictures with the probe, "Can you tell me more about your picture?"

The results of this question are still being analyzed for content; however, some interesting examples of different concepts of time are shown here to illustrate the potential of this instrument. Four broad types of responses—nothing, words only, lines, and pictures—were apparent in the responses. These are examples from the lines and picture categories of responses.

Figure 4.1a, drawn by a 38-year-old Taiwanese male was a common response. Time was measured by three years along a horizontal axis and the vertical axis was explained as "Continue advancement, better work, better life, better income." Figure 4.1b was drawn as a bar graph by a 34-year-old man from the People's Republic of China who used years and months as the horizontal axis and explained the vertical axis as "After working for a certain time, I would be promoted to a new position." About half of the line drawings from the People's Republic of China used time as the horizontal axis, the other half drew time as the vertical axis. One person drew a horizontal line labeled with positions extending forward and backward bisected by a vertical line labeled, "before joining the company and after joining the company", which was the only time dimension in the drawing. Figure 4.1c was drawn by a 30-year-old Japanese woman. It has only a label of "when I started" and "present" for time and event labels, but the picture indicates a clear work career rhythm punctuated by a family career rhythm.

One image not illustrated here, drawn by a man from the People's Republic of China also indicated a punctuated rhythm, but in this case the steps and dips were used to indicate both status and moves from one sector of the economy to another. First he worked for the army, then he worked in a state-owned enterprise, and his current job is in an entrepreneur-owned stock company in the market economy. In the explanation portion of the questionnaire he drew a spiral with no words. The line drawings used spirals, circles, and oscillations all included some passage of time as part of the labels or descriptions but none of the

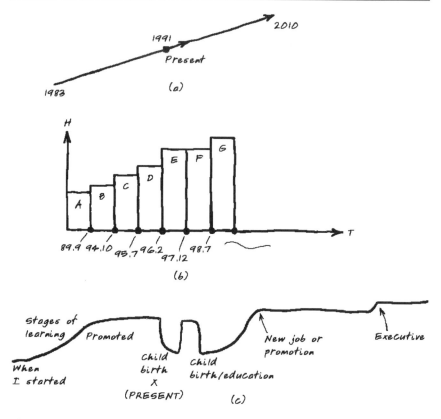

**Figure 4.1** Linear images of careers

circular drawings specified time units. One picture of a spiral, not illustrated here, was drawn by a 28-year-old Japanese woman. She described the vertical axis as time and the image as "getting concentrated toward my goals".

Figure 4.2a, from a 40-year-old Taiwanese marketing director demonstrated career rhythm and polychronicity as he combined functional growth, social development of peers and subordinates, and his own growth—a complexity of conceptualization rarely captured by standard methods, but the units of time were not labeled. He said, "Doubtlessly, responsibility should extend further as careers extend, but functional authority should not extend linearly. In the interim of functional authority expansion, a person should have a chance to refuel for the next phase of taking more functional authority." Oscillating linear images were more common in Thailand than in the other nations studied. Figure 4.2b drawn by a 28-year-old Thai female marketing executive, was a

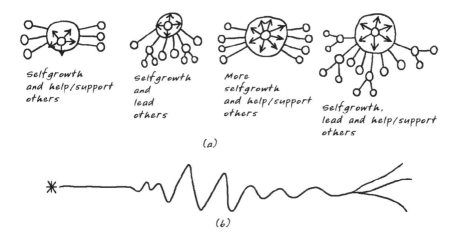

self growth
and help/support
others

self growth
and
lead
others

More
self growth
and help/support
others

self growth,
lead and help/support
others

(a)

(b)

**Figure 4.2**   Circular or wave images of careers

straight line with waves in the middle. The center section she said was, "Now—the good and bad" in the interview. She wrote, "There are many things happening in the learning process. When they all come to one point in time, one can see them clearly and work it through. . . . Of course there will be a mixture of good experiences and mistakes to learn. As time goes by, problems will be solved and cleared and finally I'll meet my goal."

The pictorial images were the most engaging responses and often they included mountains, cars, houses, and roads. A Taiwanese 55-year-old male vice-president of purchasing who drew a series of mountain peaks (Figure 4.3a) explained, "These are famous mountains in the People's Republic of China. I was told of these mountains ever since I was a child. They mean the goal or target is to do the best work you can for getting to the point." A similar but more elaborate picture drawn by a 28-year-old woman from the People's Republic of China included both the mountains and a bridge over a stream. She said, "My prospects are climbing up, that is to get career promotions occasionally. Now, I am just walking on the road leading to the bridge. The mountain lies at the end of the bridge. The mountain is my goal. . . ." Neither picture had units of time indicated, although time clearly passed in the narratives.

The example illustrated in Figure 4.3b had no written description, but in the interview, the 39-year-old Thai director described each person in her image. She said the first had ponytails and symbolized herself when she was young and naive. The second showed her growing up a little bit.

(a)

(b)

**Figure 4.3**   Picture images of careers

The third was today when she was more established with a bigger body, but still retaining a bit of ponytail because she was still inexperienced. The final image she claimed was herself five years from now, satisfied, mature, knowing everything—older and wiser. In this example the unit of time was human maturation, not a specific number of years.

This research was not designed to look at career time specifically so questions that might have yielded more time-relevant answers were not asked. In additions, we do not have enough respondents from each nation to make valid cross-national comparisons, but the responses do illustrate different ways of thinking about time and careers that might be used as stimuli for future cross-cultural studies.

Possible advantages of the draw-a-career picture technique are:

- It offers the opportunity to avoid lines altogether for cultures where linear thinking is not the mode.
- Drawings can be analyzed by members of the cultural group of the artist without using the verbal explanations (although the explanations proved most illuminating).
- It offers the chance to depict careers in both space and time.

Disadvantages are:

- It is difficult to generate a measurement and coding scheme.
- Verbal labels must be translated.
- The cultural context must be taken into account in order to identify culturally appropriate meanings for accurate analysis within a culture and for comparison across cultures.

## Draw a Career Cognitive Map

There is another alternative that has not been published as a measurement technique for career time, but might also be used to explore this idea. Cognitive maps, more popularly known as mind maps, are an emerging technique advocated to develop creativity and to describe conceptual causal processes (Markoczy & Goldberg 1995; Wycoff 1991). In mind mapping, a domain is defined as a central idea and lines are drawn that represent a series of links, connections, and mental associations to the central core idea. Rudolph (1999) has used this technique to get participants to describe how constructs related to organizational change are causally related to each other for change agents and change recipients. She found that both maps and narratives of the meaning of the maps were useful and distinct types of data.

The stimuli used to elicit cognitive maps may range from open-ended questions such as, ''How do you see your career?'' to creativity tools, ''Imagine all the possibilities for your future . . .'' to identifying links between a given set of career concepts, ''Can you locate and link these ideas: career plans, career goals, career satisfaction, career management, career success?''

Some advantages of the mind map methodology are:

- It can illustrate related ideas on one page.
- A map can be easily modified or extended by one or multiple users.
- It enables one to view the whole picture and smaller details simultaneously.
- Maps represent at least two and perhaps three dimensions of time and space.

Obvious disadvantages include problems similar to those of career pictures—deciding how to measure a map, selecting domains to compare one map with another, and translating verbal labels to concepts of equivalent meanings. Only some of the techniques of mind mapping would be suitable for measuring units of time in addition to measuring units of cognitive space. In spite of the problems, interpreting mind maps within a particular cultural context and comparing mind maps drawn by members of different cultures offers at least one other novel way to move beyond our current methodologies to include alternative views of reality about career time.

## CONCLUSIONS

If we consider the survey technique, the draw-a-line technique, the draw-a-picture technique and the draw-a-map technique, we see that it is impossible to escape the need for interpreting any method of description or measurement within the cultural context of the respondents. It is also impossible to escape the problem of trying to identify whether or not there are equivalent units of time measurement in different cultures. What these drawing methodologies add to the traditional forms of scales and surveys is the option to move in two or three dimensions and to encourage non-verbal expressions which might be particularly appropriate for illustrating a concept of time that is different from a US unilinear, unidirectional concept of time.

There are many directions for future research using these techniques. Questions of how people in different organizational cultures, as well as different ethnic cultures, view the various dimensions of time remain to be answered. The conception of time as a point of the present around which other things oscillate is the most distant from current discussions of time in careers literature but, for that reason alone, it warrants further cross-cultural exploration. Exploring different units of time also offers new avenues of cross-cultural understanding. In the career picture example, units of measurement included calendar years and months, age, human maturational stages, specific events such as joining a firm or moving from one firm to another, or a single point in the present. Those concerned about organizational effectiveness might well wonder whether members of different sub-units of a multinational firm, or workers in different departments, or members of different ethnic groups in a domestic enterprise, are operating on similar or different conceptualizations of career time, reward time, and productivity time. Those most interested in preserving a safe and sustainable world for future generations might want to ask how career concepts of time common in countries of reincarnation could be applied to environmental responsibility issues in the United States and Europe. Work–family scholars and practitioners could use these techniques to describe and analyze the synchronicity and entrainment of multiple career processes of couples in a marriage or groups of employees within organizations.

The work content connected with the images of careers were growth, status, positions, joy, sweat, goals, income, and responsibility. They also offer intriguing avenues for further research. What do people think about when they think about their careers? How are these concepts connected in their minds? Are these concepts connected to valued rewards or stumbling blocks to developing new organizational contracts between employees and employers? How long might those contracts be extended into the future in different firms and in different locations?

Some will surely argue that we should stick with words and numbers as more "precise" ways to measure any phenomenon in one or many cultures. It is possible to apply words and numbers to all of these methods (distance ratios from network analysis have been used). However, this argument perpetuates a particular form of ethnocentrism as well as a particular form of positivist management science belief in the precision of objective measurement science that is not as common in qualitative techniques used in other research domains and in other geographic locations. If scholars and practitioners wish to capture many dimensions of subjective perceptions of career time in a range of different cultures we need to try multiple methodologies. The more methods that are explored, the more likely it is that we will be able to capture a more complete picture of the complex career reality as seen through the eyes of people socialized into other cultures. The methods presented here are the tip of the iceberg, available to scholars and practitioners willing to seek alternative means to depict career time. If we ask our colleagues from other cultures to help us dig beneath the tip of that iceberg, many more methods will surface.

## REFERENCES

Agbor-Baiyee, W. (1997) A cyclic model of career motivation. *College Student Journal*, **31**(4): 467–472.

Alland, A. (1983) *Playing with Form: Children Draw in Six Cultures*. New York: Columbia University Press.

Allmendinger, J., Bruckner, H., Fuchs, S. & von Stebut, N. (1997) Between inner and outer circles: Women's careers in elite research organizations. *Sociological Abstracts*, American Sociological Association.

Althen, G. (1988) *American Ways: A Guide for Foreigners in the United States*. Yarmouth, MA: Intercultural Press.

Arthur, M. & Rousseau, D. (1996) *The Boundaryless Career*. New York: Oxford University Press.

Berry, J. W., Poortinga, Y. H., Segall, M. H. & Dasen, P. R. (1992) *Cross-Cultural Psychology: Research and Applications*. New York: Cambridge University Press.

Chow, I. H. S. (1997) Careers of Hong Kong managers. In C. S. Granrose (Ed.) *The Careers of Business Managers in East Asia* (pp. 37–66). Westport, CT: Quorum.

Dowling, P. J., Welch, D. & Schuller, R. (1999) *International Human Resources Management, 3rd edition*, Cincinnati, OH: South-Western.

Earls, A. (1998) CareerXroads. *Computerworld*, **32**(8): 86.

Frooman, J. (1999) Stakeholders influence strategies. *Academy of Management Review*, **24**(2): 191–205.

Gombrich, E. H. (1977) *Art and Illusion: A Study in the Psychology of Pictorial Representation*, 5th edn. Oxford: Phaidon Press.

Gordon, J. R. & Whelan, K. S. (1998) Successful professional women in midlife: How organizations can more effectively understand and respond to the challenges. *Academy of Management Executive*, **12**(1): 8–28.

Granrose, C. S. (1995) Career images of Asian managers. Paper presented at the annual meeting of the Academy of Management, Vancouver, BC.

Granrose, C. S., Ed. (1997) *The Careers of Business Managers in East Asia*. Westport, CT: Quorum.

Granrose, C. S. & Huang, Q. (1999) *Careers in P. R. China*. Unpublished manuscript, Claremont, CA.

Gunz, H., Jalland, R. M. & Evans, M. (1998) New strategy, wrong managers? What you need to know about career streams. *Academy of Management Executive*, **12**(2): 21–37.

Hall, D. T. (1997) Special challenges of careers in the 21st century. *Academy of Management Executive*, **11**(1): 60–61.

Hall, E. T. (1983) *The Dance of Life: The Other Dimension of Time*. Garden City, NY: Anchor Press.

Iberra, H. (1997) Paving an alternative route: Gender differences in managerial networks. *Social Psychology Quarterly*, **60**(1): 91–102.

Jassawalla, A. R. & Sashittal, H.C. (1999) Building collaborative cross-functional new product teams. *The Academy of Management Executive*, **13**(3): 50–64.

Kelley, L. & Luo, Y. D. (1999) *China 2000*. Thousand Oaks, CA: Sage.

Kluckhohn, F. R. & Strodtbeck, F. L. (1961) *Variations in Value Orientations*. Evanston, IL: Row, Peterson.

London, M. (1998) *Career Barriers: How People Experience, Overcome and Avoid Failure*. Mahway, NJ: Lawrence Erlbaum Associates.

Markoczy, L. & Goldberg, J. (1995) A method for eliciting and comparing causal maps. *Journal of Management*, **21**(2): 305–333.

McElhaney, M. (1969) *Clinical Assessment of the Human Figure Drawing*. Springfield, MA: Thomas.

McGrath, J. E. & Kelly, J. R. (1986) *Time and Human Interaction: Toward a Social Psychology of Time*. New York: Guilford Press.

Millikin, F. J., Martins, L. L. & Morgan, H. (1998) Explaining organizational responsiveness to work–family issues: The role of human resource executives as issue interpreters. *Academy of Management Journal*, **41**(5): 580–592.

Punnett, B. J. & Shenkar, O. (1996) *Handbook for International Management Research*. Cambridge, MA: Blackwell.

Rudolph, J. W. (1999) Conflicting mental models of change: An analysis of causal maps and narratives in the context of failed change efforts. Unpublished manuscript, Carroll School of Management, Boston College, Boston, MA.

Schettler, T. (Ed.), Solomon, G. M., Valenti, M. & Huddle, A. (1999) *Generations at Risk: Reproductive Health and the Environment*. Boston, MA: MIT Press.

Serpell, R. & Deregowski, J. B. (1980) The skill of pictorial perception: An interpretation of cross-cultural evidence. *International Journal of Psychology*, **15**: 145–180.

Williams, J. R. (1999) *Renewable Advantage: Crafting Strategy Through Economic Time*. New York: Free Press.

Wycoff, J. (1991) *Mindmapping: Your Personal Guide to Exploring Creativity and Problem-Solving*. Berkeley, CA: Berkeley.

Zahra, S. (1999) The changing rules of global competitiveness in the 21st century. *Academy of Management Executive*, **13**(1): 36–42.

# CHAPTER 5

# Time, Person–Career Fit, and the Boundaryless Career

Saroj Parasuraman, Jeffrey H. Greenhaus and Frank Linnehan
*Drexel University, USA*

## INTRODUCTION

The concept of time is implicitly or explicitly embedded in a number of topics related to the workplace. Although early management researchers studied time in the context of efficiency and productivity, it remains a neglected topic in much of the organizational behavior research. Time is a complex concept, with different meanings in different contexts. Researchers in the social sciences view time as a mechanism by which social institutions segment activities into precise temporal units, and condition individuals to organized "time consciousness" (Hassard 1991).

Time and its many dimensions enter into different elements of the employment relationship between individuals and organizations. Work schedules such as the five-day, 40-hour work week and the three-shift, around-the-clock operation are examples of the time-structuring of organizations and individuals. The total number of hours worked per week is used to classify employees as full-time or part-time. Work that exceeds the normal working hours has been described as "overtime" if required by the employer, and may be eligible for additional compensation. Time also determines the mode of compensation (hourly or salaried), and eligibility for employer-sponsored benefits, as well as the continuity and security of employment (Fisher, Schoenfeldt & Shaw 1999).

Prominent among the many properties of time is the fact that it is fixed and immutable. Hence, time is viewed as a scarce resource to be managed

*Trends in Organizational Behavior*, Volume 7. Edited by C. L. Cooper and D. M. Rousseau.
Copyright © 2000 John Wiley & Sons, Ltd.

carefully (Bluedorn & Denhardt 1988; Hassard 1991). Non-attendance at work is described as "time lost" and is usually measured by the number of days an individual is absent from work over a period of time (Chadwick-Jones, Brown, C. A., Nicholson, N., & Sheppard, C. 1971).

The passage of time has also been treated as an indicator or proxy for a variety of work-related phenomena. Thus, organizational tenure has traditionally been interpreted as an indicator of employee loyalty or commitment to the organization. Additionally, the number of hours spent per week at work is regarded both as a behavioral indicator of career and organizational commitment as well as of high performance, reflecting the importance of "face time" in organizational settings (Christensen 1997). In contrast, length of time spent in the same job with no added responsibility is generally regarded as a sign of career plateauing with limited prospects for upward mobility.

Despite the many ways in which the concept of time has been incorporated into the study of various organizational phenomena, there is surprisingly little research examining time and temporal factors explicitly in the organizational literature. It is only relatively recently that organizational researchers have recognized this void and called for research examining the role of time in diverse aspects of organizational behavior (Bluedorn & Denhardt 1988. Hassard 1991; Katz 1980).

This chapter examines the role of time in shaping individuals' career experiences, and traces the changes in the implications of time that have accompanied recent shifts in the meaning of a career. First, we discuss the ways in which the passage of time has been incorporated into the traditional view of an organizational career. Next, we explore the properties of evolving alternative careers represented in the "boundaryless career" (Arthur 1994), and review differences in the time horizons within organizational careers and boundaryless careers. We then explore the concept of person–career fit, and conclude with the development of a model that depicts three patterns of changes in person–career fit over the life-course.

## TIME AND THE ORGANIZATIONAL CAREER

Time occupies a central role in career theory. The importance of time is illustrated abundantly in theoretical models of careers that typically take a life-course perspective on the work experiences of individuals. In a review of career-related articles published in inter-disciplinary journals during the 1980s and early 1990s, Arthur (1994) found that some discussion of time was common to every article. Time is the key element that differentiates a job from a career, a distinction widely accepted until the 1970s. Whereas a career was considered to involve a long-term goal and consisted of a sequence of planned moves up the organizational hierarchy, a job was regarded as merely employment and an *ad hoc* work experience. Careers were also thought to include professional work, hierarchical advancement, and occupational stability as essential characteristics (Greenhaus, Callanan & Godshalk 2000).

Contemporary conceptualizations of a career are broader and less restrictive. Hall's (1976, p. 4) definition of a career as "an individually perceived sequence of attitudes and behaviors associated with work-related experiences and activities over the span of the person's life" was among the first to drop the constraints of professionalism, advancement, and stability. A recent and widely accepted definition describes a career as the "evolving sequence of a person's work experiences over time" (Arthur, Hall & Lawrence 1989, p. 8). Similar definitions of a career have been offered by Feldman (1988) and Greenhaus *et al.* (2000).

Despite these broadened conceptualizations of a career, the notion of pursuing a career *within a single organization* has persisted throughout much of the twentieth century, especially for men. The economic prosperity ushered in after World War II stimulated growth and generated tremendous demand for human capital (Callanan & Greenhaus 1999). To attract and retain productive employees, organizations promised job security and opportunities for continued advancement in exchange for loyalty to the organization on the part of the employee (Nicholson 1996; Robinson, Kraatz & Rousseau 1994; Rousseau & Wade-Benzoni 1995). The psychological contract between employee and employer was "relational" in nature, and provided a sense of long-term security and stability to both parties (MacNeill 1985). Not surprisingly, many employees aspired to spend all, or nearly all, of their career with the same organization, and the organization in turn reciprocated with recognition and gold watches for longevity of employment.

The concept of an organizational career has also been inextricably linked to the passage of time and stages in the life cycle of individuals. Career experiences of individuals were believed to involve distinct stages of development that assume a set of predictable work experiences pursued within one occupation if not one organization. Such stages as exploration, establishment, advancement, maintenance, and decline (Hall & Nougaim 1968; Super 1980) were assumed to be universal among all employees, with individuals passing through each stage of development only once as their careers unfolded. Schein's influential model of career development—with its demarcations of early career, mid career, and late career—is based on "a model of what a career would look like if pursued fully and successfully" (Schein 1978, p. 37).

These early conceptualizations of career development were generally consistent with the reality of the times because many employees did spend a large part of their adult life within one occupation and even in one organization. Each stage of career development unfolded over a long period of time (typically 10–20 or more years) and presented specific tasks and challenges that required the attention of the employee. Consequently, there were relatively few major career transitions that occurred between these lengthy career stages.

It should be noted that the traditional view of careers did not reflect the career experiences of women. Early career theories were predicated on the assumption that men were the primary breadwinners and careers were mostly pursued by men for whom work was believed to be a central life interest. In this view of careers, men were able to devote inordinate amounts of time to the work role due to the presence of a non-employed spouse who assumed almost total responsibility for home maintenance and childcare. The careers of women (especially those who are married and have children) were typically characterized by discontinuities in employment, periods of part-time employment, and career interruptions due to childbirth, parenting demands, or involuntary moves related to the spouse's career (Arthur, Inkson & Pringle 1999; Parasuraman & Greenhaus 1993).

The assumed predictable sequence and timing of career stages enabled individuals to assess their career success in terms of the level in the organizational hierarchy they had reached by a certain age. Lawrence (1984) discussed the process of "age grading" in organizations and observed how individuals determine whether they are on-schedule, ahead of schedule, or behind schedule in their accomplishments. Indeed, the whole concept of a "fast track" represents an attempt to accelerate the experiences and accomplishments of select high-potential managers. Alternatively, being behind schedule is interpreted as having reached a career plateau, "the point in a career where the likelihood of additional hierarchical promotion is very low" (Ference, Stoner & Warren 1977, p. 602).

This traditional view of an organizational career was based on the assumption of steady growth in the economy and relative stability in organizations' internal and external environments. However, social, economic, technological, and cultural changes during the last two decades have radically altered the nature of work and the workforce, necessitating changes in the organization of work and the nature of careers, and the consequent revision of theories of career development. We now examine an alternative career perspective and discuss its implications for time over the life-course.

## TIME AND THE BOUNDARYLESS CAREER

The 1980s and 1990s have witnessed the emergence of alternative perspectives on the meaning of a career. No longer tied or "bounded" to a single employer or even to one occupation, individuals' careers are increasingly viewed as boundaryless in nature (Arthur 1994), with nearly all careers crossing multiple employer boundaries (Arthur, Inkson & Pringle 1999). The concept of the boundaryless career evolved in response to fundamental changes in organizational structures and processes. Global competitive pressures and the need to be more flexible and innovative have led to the ongoing downsizing and restructuring of organizations and a shift toward becoming leaner, flatter, and more customer-driven (DeFillippi & Arthur 1994).

Working with only a small core staff and a larger group of temporary contract and contingent employees, boundaryless organizations use cross-functional teams extensively to respond more quickly and effectively to changes in the marketplace (Byrne 1993). These organizations are boundaryless in the sense that the borders between functional areas, between hierarchical levels, and between the organization and its suppliers of physical, informational, and human resources have become increasingly permeable.

Perhaps the most significant change within the boundaryless organization is the replacement of the old relational psychological contract between employer and employee by a more transactional contract. The short-term nature of the transactional contract enables organizations to change directions rapidly in response to changes in the marketplace. In this still-evolving contract, the employee's contribution is not loyalty, but rather the acquisition of a portfolio of skills that are required by the organization at a particular point in time (Arthur *et al.* 1999). This requires organizations to invest in the development of human capital and individuals to develop diverse new skills when needed.

In return, the organization does not provide the promise of continued employment—as in a relational contract—but rather opportunities for the employee to develop new skills and become employable or marketable either in the current organization or in a different firm (Waterman, Waterman & Collard 1994). Moreover, the organization no longer promises rapid advancement up the hierarchy. Work assignments are more temporary and project-based, career paths—to the extent that they exist—are more unpredictable, and mobility in such organizations is more likely to be horizontal than vertical. However, career paths today are also more likely to be characterized by mobility across companies, rather than within a single company. In their study of the career paths of 75 employees in nine occupational categories, Arthur *et al.* (1999) found that the proportion of mobile employees who made inter-company moves was nearly four times (79 per cent) that of employees who made intra-company moves (21 per cent). The moves across organizational boundaries involved not only a change of employer, but also of industry, occupation, and geographic location. In addition, most of the voluntary inter-organizational moves did not involve conventional career advancement in terms of higher levels of responsibility, status, or pay.

Boundaryless careers are pursued within this changing landscape of work. This destabilization of the organization has led to the subsequent decoupling of careers from organizational structures. Boundaryless careers are self-directed paths cutting across less formal organizational and extra-organizational boundaries (Arthur 1994; Arthur, Inkson & Pringle 1999; DeFillippi & Arthur 1994).

In the traditional organizational career, stages of development were typically based on chronological age. Employees explored options, chose an occupation, established themselves in the field, rose in the organizational hierarchy, plateaued, and ultimately declined and disengaged from work. In the boundaryless career, stages or cycles of development are likely to repeat themselves many times over the course of one's work life. The stages are of shorter duration because of the number and frequency of major changes that require adaptation and learning (Arthur, Inkson and Pringle 1999; Hall & Mirvis 1995). Frequent moves across projects, companies, industries, or even occupations create shorter cycles of exploration, establishment, advancement, maintenance, and decline. Similarly, moving between full-time employment and part-time employment, between work and sabbatical, or between organizational employment and self-employment produces more frequent cycles of shorter duration—and more frequent career transitions.

These transitions have been viewed as "prevailing cycles of change and adaptation", each of which requires "preparation, encounter, adjustment, stabilization, and renewed preparation" (Arthur & Rousseau 1996, p. 33). Mirvis and Hall (1994) view these cycles as periods of re-skilling, and introduce the notion of "career age" (rather than chronological age) to capture an individual's progress through a particular career cycle.

Whereas advancement in the traditional organizational career was more predictably linked to an organization's timetable, flatter, boundaryless organizations provide fewer opportunities for advancement, and the route to advancement may require many lateral moves, and some seemingly downward changes. In addition, there can be disruptions to orderly and predictable advancement because of radical changes to an organization's strategy or structure (e.g. acquisitions, outsourcing of functions). Furthermore, because an individual may shift between core and temporary worker, between part-time and full-time employment, between one company and another, it is difficult to determine whether one is on schedule. In fact, there may not be one schedule but rather many variations of schedules.

As a result, the recent literature has directed attention away from viewing rapid upward, linear progression through an organization as the sole—

or primary—indicator of career success. The reliance on external guides for sequences of work experience has given way to the use of internal self-generated guides such as growth, learning, and integration. Career growth is increasingly measured by feelings of psychological success derived from achieving personally important goals (Hall 1996; Mirvis & Hall 1994), as well as by the development of skills, competence, and experience (Weick 1996) that can enhance the individual's marketability. This perspective has served not only to focus careers research on individual characteristics, attitudes and motives, but also to disconnect careers and career success from organizations and hierarchies (Arthur & Rousseau 1996).

Table 5.1 summarizes and compares the key properties of the boundary-less model with those of the organizational career model and differentiates

**Table 5.1** The relationship between time and key dimensions of organizational and boundaryless careers

| Dimension | Organizational | Boundaryless | Time horizons |
|---|---|---|---|
| Focus | Career | Jobs/projects | Long term vs. short term |
| Career stages | Chronological age coincides with career stages of fixed duration and sequence | No relationship between career cycles and chronological age. Cycles are variable in duration | Fixed vs. variable |
| Mobility | Linear, upward, hierarchical | Lateral and non-hierarchical, intra- and inter-organizational moves | Infrequent vs. frequent |
| Identification with work | Single organization or occupation | Multiple organizations and occupations | Long term vs. short term |
| Rewards criteria | Seniority, long-term achievement and potential | Short-term, demonstrated results | Total career vs. immediate accomplishments |
| Career success (individual perspective) | On/ahead of perceived organizational schedule | Psychological success and continued development | Organizationally defined timetable vs. personal timetable |
| Career success (organizational perspective) | Job performance and face time. Salary, rank and position in hierarchy | Deliverable results and growth in personal identity and adaptability | Duration: long vs. short |

the models on the basis of their orientation to time. The presence of repeated career cycles over the course of an individual's work life—and the emergence of the concept of career age to depict one's development through each cycle—raises a number of interesting issues regarding career development over the life span. In the next section, we propose a model of life-long career transitions to stimulate theory development and empirical research.

## A MODEL OF LIFE-LONG CAREER TRANSITIONS

The representation of a boundaryless career as a series of frequent cycles of relatively short duration raises two important questions that suggest new avenues for theory and research. First, does the *sequence* of career cycles form a larger pattern of development over the life-course? Despite the significance of the concept of career age, we believe that chronological age can also help us understand the evolution of career cycles in boundaryless careers. We propose that there may be overarching patterns of development *across* career cycles and that an individual's age—and the associated growth in experience and wisdom—plays a role in determining the pattern. Moreover, as we discuss below, we believe that Levinson's (1986) concept of adult life development may help us understand the pattern of career cycles across the life span.

Secondly, if career cycles form a larger pattern over the life-course, in what ways do cycles vary over time? Hall's (1996) model of learning stages identifies changes in an individual's job performance from one cycle to the next. Although job performance is relevant to individuals and their employers, we believe that the degree of fit or congruence between personal characteristics and career experiences may be an especially useful perspective to examine changes in career cycles across the life-course.

Person–career fit, being a cornerstone of many career decision-making theories, is the extent to which an individual's career experiences are compatible with his or her needs, values, interests, and talents. Individuals generally choose career fields that are compatible with these personal qualities and therefore represent an expression of the self-concept. Moreover, because a high degree of fit can promote positive work attitudes and stability in a career field (Blau 1987; Smart, Elton & McLaughlin 1986; Spokane 1985), it is considered an important indicator of career effectiveness (Betz, Fitzgerald & Hill 1989). Although person–career fit is usually achieved through the selection of a job or career field that is compatible with personal qualities, it is also likely that individuals can proactively change their work environment—what Weick (1996) has referred to as enactment—to achieve greater fit.

The model presented in Figure 5.1 portrays the career as a series of cycles that unfold over the span of an individual's life. By reconnecting age and careers, and coupling them with the concept of person–career fit, the model helps to identify transitional career patterns that may emerge over an individual's life. Each career cycle is represented by a circle, the diameter of which depicts the duration of the cycle. Although not shown in the diagram, each cycle contains the developmental tasks of exploration, trial, establishment, and mastery (Hall 1996; Mirvis & Hall 1994). The overlap between some of the circles is indicative of the overlap that can occur across career cycles, i.e. the completion of one cycle can lay the groundwork for the initiation of the subsequent cycle. Finally, the arrows represent the career movements that occur between cycles.

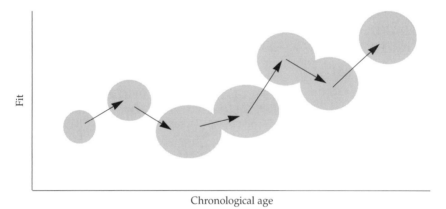

**Figure 5.1**   Model of life-long career transitions: increasing levels of person–career fit over time. ● represents career cycle, which includes progression through career stages (exploration, trial, establishment, and mastery); ⟶ career transition

The horizontal axis of Figure 5.1 represents chronological age, and the vertical axis represents the degree of person–career fit. Figure 5.1 indicates that career cycles generally display an increasing level of person–career fit over the course of an individual's life. This is an ideal pattern of development because it suggests that individuals enhance their capacity to achieve fit over time. However, some individuals may display a random pattern of person–career fit as they get older, and others may witness a decline in fit over time (Figures 5.2 and 5.3 respectively). We next discuss the factors that may differentiate these three sequences of career cycles.

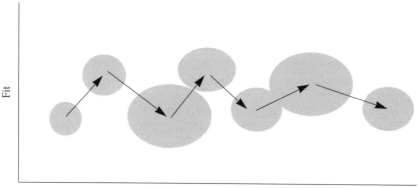

Chronological age

**Figure 5.2**   Model of life-long career transitions: random changes in person–career fit over time. ● represents career cycle, which includes progression through career stages (exploration, trial, establishment, and mastery); ➤ career transition

Fit

Chronological age

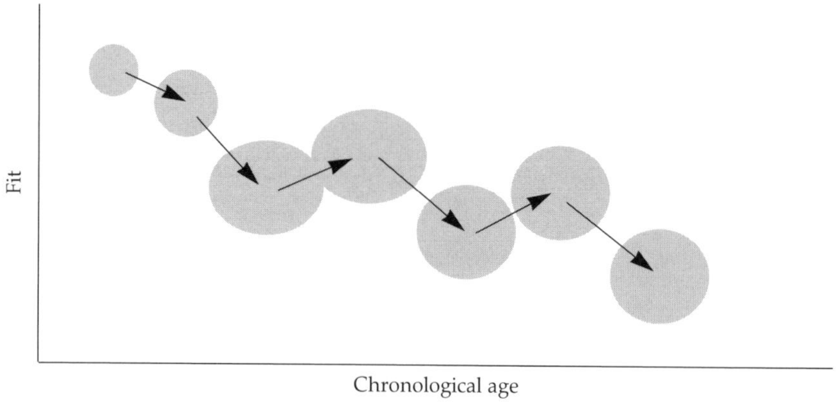

**Figure 5.3**   Model of life-long career transitions: declining levels of person–career fit over time. ● represents career cycle, which includes progression through career stages (exploration, trial, establishment, and mastery); ➤ career transition

We expect that some—perhaps many—individuals will achieve increasingly higher levels of person–career fit over the course of a lifetime, due to growth in their experience, maturity, and career competencies. This positive relationship between age and fit does not imply that each career cycle will necessarily produce a higher level of fit than the immediately preceding cycle. Figure 5.1 shows that cycles of lower fit are occasionally interspersed with general increases in fit over time.

It has been suggested that boundaryless careers require three types of career competencies (Arthur, Claman & DeFillippi 1995). Employees need to understand themselves to determine whether they fit the culture of their organization ("knowing why" competencies). They also must add to their repertoire of skills to maintain their job performance and reputation ("knowing how"), and must cultivate a broad array of relationships inside and outside the organization ("knowing whom"). In a similar vein, Hall (1996) (see also Mirvis & Hall 1994) emphasizes the importance of two meta-skills necessary to experience psychological success over time: the development of personal identity and adaptability.

Following, Hall & Mirvis (1995), we assume that career competencies and meta-skills can increase as individuals get older, acquire more extensive experience, and achieve greater maturity. Employees who learn from their experiences should develop greater insight into themselves and work environments as their career experiences accumulate over time. They can also expand their portfolio of skills, extend their network of relationships, and appreciate the benefits of adaptability as they move from cycle to cycle throughout their lives.

These age-related career competencies and meta-skills are likely to steer individuals toward new career cycles that have the capacity to satisfy their personal needs and values and utilize their talents. The better we understand ourselves, the more capably we assess work environments, and the more extensively we utilize networks, the more likely we are to pursue and select jobs and assignments that are compatible with our self-concept. In effect, these competencies enable individuals to make "vigilant" career decisions that are based on a deep understanding of oneself and one's options (Greenhaus et al. 2000). Moreover, heightened insight and greater adaptability should enable individuals to modify their work environment when necessary to achieve greater fit.

This pattern of increasing person–career fit over the life-course, however, requires more than the acquisition of career competencies and skills. It also demands sufficiently high self-esteem for individuals to pursue situations that are capable of satisfying their needs (Korman 1976). High self-esteem employees are likely to utilize their competencies to achieve increasing fit over the course of their career because they are motivated to meet their needs and confirm their positive self-concept. Low self-esteem employees, whose self-concept is threatened by success, are not expected to display increasing levels of fit as they progress through life.

Moreover, individuals who place moderate or substantial importance on the work role are more likely to achieve increasing person–career fit over the lifetime than individuals who place minimal importance on work. Work-salient individuals tend to be proactive in career management (Sugalski & Greenhaus 1986), which can promote effective career decision-making. If work takes a back seat to other life roles, then individuals may not be highly motivated to seek career situations that are compatible with their needs, values, interests, and talents.

In summary, the pattern of increasing fit over the lifetime requires (1) the competencies and skills to make effective career decisions and (2) the motivation to satisfy one's career needs derived from high self-esteem and a salient work role. If any of these ingredients are substantially lacking, then other patterns of fit may emerge. For example, Figure 5.2 reveals an apparently random pattern of person–career fit over the life-course. Increases in fit from one cycle to the next are as likely to be followed by subsequent declines in fit as by further increases. We speculate that this pattern is due to a number of factors. First, it is possible that individuals have not fully developed their career competencies as they have gotten older. They may not have learned from their prior experiences what they want from work or how to assess career opportunities as a source of congruence or fit. Their occasional increases in fit from one cycle to the next may be due more to serendipity than to any proactive efforts or skill on their part.

It is also possible that many of their career moves have been driven by external factors. Time and economic pressures often accompany involuntary or externally driven career moves. Employees who lose their jobs due to an organizational downsizing or a divestiture may not have made adequate financial preparations for an extended period of time without income. Thus, it is likely that externally driven transitions result in career decisions based purely on economic factors with little consideration of compatibility or fit with a wide range of values or needs. Moreover, individuals who experience high levels of anxiety in their career may panic at the need to make a quick decision and therefore make a hasty, ill-conceived "hypervigilant" decision to relieve their stress (Greenhaus *et al.* 2000).

Conversely, internally driven transitions may not produce the same time or financial urgency as those precipitated by factors outside the control of the individual. These transitions are more likely to be based on the individual's own timetable and a greater knowledge of the consequences of the choice that is being made. This allows the individual more time to prepare for the change both psychologically and financially. Therefore, the pattern of internally and externally driven transitions can help explain changes in fit over time.

The pattern of declining fit over a lifetime (Figure 5.3) is more difficult to explain. Such situations—which are hopefully not commonplace—may reflect a vicious cycle of failure and pessimism that drastically erodes self-esteem, which, in turn, can decrease feelings of competence and involvement in the career role (Hall 1976). Thus, they invest less of themselves in making career decisions as they get older, and the poor quality of these decisions reinforces their low self-esteem and aversion to work.

So far, the models we have presented have addressed changes in the *level* of person–career fit achieved over time. It is possible that the elements that comprise fit also change during the life-course. An individual can make career decisions to satisfy primarily work-related values (e.g. money, status, challenge, advancement, responsibility), or can make decisions based also on a variety of work, family, and personal values (Greenhaus *et al.* 2000) by expanding their sense of self (Mirvis & Hall 1994). Some individuals—perhaps in increasing numbers—make career decisions that are intended to bring balance between their work and other parts of their lives. Others focus narrowly on the implications of their career decisions solely for their work life.

We propose that self-initiated career transitions during middle adulthood and late adulthood are more likely to involve the search for work–life balance than transitions during early adulthood. According to Levinson (1986), the main tasks of early adulthood are to find a niche for oneself in adult society and to pursue a "dream", an intense view of how one wants to live his or her life. This often requires individuals to establish priorities in order to achieve substantial success in the dominant focus of their lives, the objects of their dreams. The early career generally involves an intense career focus as individuals attempt to establish themselves and demonstrate their competence to their employers and themselves. Therefore, we propose that the aim of career decisions during early adulthood is primarily to achieve fit with an individual's significant work needs, values, interests, and talents.

Middle adulthood involves a re-examination of the decisions and accomplishments and/or failures of early adulthood and a subsequent attempt to fashion a satisfactory lifestyle for the middle years of one's life. Late adulthood requires a reappraisal of the previous era and an effort to achieve a sense of integrity regarding one's entire life. Because of the importance of "wholeness" and integrity in middle and late adulthood, we predict that career decisions during these eras of adult life development are driven by the need to achieve a broader type of fit that includes balance among significant life roles.

## CONCLUSIONS

Our exploration of the concept of time in relation to organizational behavior demonstrates that time occupies a central role in theoretical models of careers and career development over the course of individuals' working lives. Our analysis and interpretation of the key characteristics of careers indicate that time is a critical factor that differentiates organizational or traditional careers from the still evolving, boundaryless career. We found that the frequency, duration, and timing of events are relevant to a better understanding of variations in career cycles over time. We identified the notion of fit or congruence between career experiences and personal characteristics as a useful perspective to examine the pattern of relationships between career cycles. Coupling the concept of fit with age and career cycles, we propose a model that posits the likelihood of increasing fit over the life-course as individuals gain experience, mature, and develop new competencies. We also present alternative scenarios that explain the possibility of declining fit or a random pattern of fit over time.

We hope that our model will stimulate scholarly discussions and additional research on different aspects of time and its relationship to careers. We encourage researchers interested in career development to undertake empirical research to develop operational measures that capture the various dimensions and meanings of time in the world of careers. It would also be useful to assess whether there are differences in the pattern of long-term fit between individuals who occupy core roles and those who occupy more temporary positions in boundaryless organizations. Finally, we call on researchers in international careers to examine differences in the role of time in careers that cross national boundaries, and the impact of such differences on the pathways to career success and satisfaction across cultures.

## REFERENCES

Arthur, M. B. (1994) The boundaryless career: a new perspective for organizational inquiry. *Journal of Organizational Behavior*, **15**: 295–306.

Arthur, M. B. & Rousseau, D. M. (1996) A career lexicon for the 21st century. *Academy of Management Executive*, **10**: 28–39.

Arthur, M. B., Claman, P. H., & De Fillippi, R. J. (1995) Intelligent enterprise, intelligent careers. *Academy of Management Executive*, **9**, 7–20.

Arthur, M. B., Hall, D. T. & Lawrence, B. S. (1989) Generating new directions in career theory: the case for a transdisciplinary approach. In M. B. Arthur, D. T. Hall & B. S. Lawrence (Eds) *Handbook of Career Theory* (pp. 7–25). Cambridge, UK: Cambridge University Press.

Arthur, M. B., Inkson, K. & Pringle, J. K. (1999) *The New Careers Individual Action and Economic Change*. Thousand Oaks, CA: Sage.

Betz, N. E., Fitzgerald, L. F. & Hill. R. E. (1989) Trait–factor theory: traditional cornerstone of career theory. In M. B. Arthur, D. T. Hall & B. S. Lawrence (Eds) *Handbook of Career Theory* (pp. 26–40). Cambridge, UK: Cambridge University Press.

Blau, G. J. (1987) Using a person–environment fit model to predict job involvement and organizational commitment. *Journal of Vocational Behavior*, **30**: 240–257.

Bluedorn, A. C. & Denhardt, R. B. (1988) Time and organizations. *Journal of Management*, **14**: 289–311.

Byrne, J. A. (1993) The horizontal corporation. *Business Week*, **20 December**: 76–81.

Callanan, G. A. & Greenhaus, J. H. (1999) Personal and career development. In A. I. Kraut & A. K. Korman (Eds), *Evolving Practices in Human Resource Management: Response to a Changing World* (pp. 146–171). San Francisco: Jossey-Bass.

Chadwick-Jones, J. K., Brown, C. A., Nicholson, N. & Sheppard, C. (1971) Absence measures: Their reliability and stability in an industrial setting. *Personnel Psychology*, **24**: 463–470.

Christensen, P. M. (1997) Toward a comprehensive work/life strategy. In S. Parasuraman & J. H. Greenhaus (Eds), *Integrating Work and Family: Challenges and Choices for a Changing World* (pp. 25–37). Westport, CT: Quorum.

DeFillippi, R. J. & Arthur, M. B. (1994) The boundaryless career: a competency-based perspective. *Journal of Organizational Behavior*, **15**: 307–324.

Feldman, D. C. (1988) *Managing Careers in Organizations*. Glenview, IL: Scott Foresman.

Ference, T. P., Stoner, J. A. F. & Warren, E. K. (1977) Managing the career plateau. *Academy of Management Review*, **2**: 602–612.

Fisher. C. D., Schoenfeldt. L. F. & Shaw, J. B. (1999) *Human Resource Management*, 4th edn. Boston, MA: Houghton Mifflin.

Greenhaus, J. H. *et al.* (2000) *Career Management*, 3rd edn. Fort Worth, TX: The Dryden Press.

Hall, D. T. (1976) *Careers in Organizations*. Glenview, IL: Scott Foresman.

Hall, D. T. (1996) Protean careers of the 21st century. *Academy of Management Executive*, **10**: 8–16.

Hall, D. T. & Mirvis, P. H. (1995) The new career contract: Developing the whole person at midlife and beyond. *Journal of Vocational Behavior*, **47**: 269–289.

Hall, D. T. & Nougaim, K. (1968) An examination of Maslow's need hierarchy in an organizational setting. *Organizational Behavior and Human Performance*, **3**: 12–35.

Hassard, J. (1991) Aspects of time in organizations. *Human Relations*, **44**: 105–136.

Katz, R. (1980) Time and work: Toward an integrative perspective. In B. M. Staw & L. L. Cummings (Eds), *Research in Organizational Behavior* (Vol. 2, pp. 81–128). Greenwich, CT: JAI Press.

Korman, A. K. (1976) An hypothesis of work behavior revisited and an extension. *Academy of Management Review*, **1**: 50–63.

Lawrence, B. S. (1984) Age grading: the implicit organizational timetable. *Journal of Occupational Behaviour*, **5**: 23–35.

Levinson, D. J. (1986) A concept of adult development. *American Psychologist*, **41**, 3–13.

MacNeill, I. R. (1985) Relational contracts: what we do and do not know. *Wisconsin Law Review*, **3**: 483–525.

Mirvis, P. H. & Hall, D. T. (1994) Psychological success and the boundaryless career. *Journal of Organizational Behavior*, **15**: 365–380.

Nicholson, N. (1996) Career systems in crisis: change and opportunity in the information age. *Academy of Management Executive*, **10**: 40–51.

Parasuraman, S. & Greenhaus, J. H. (1993) Personal portrait: the lifestyle of the woman manager. In E. A. Fagenson (Ed.), *Women in Management: Trends, Issues and Challenges in Managerial Diversity* (Vol. 4). Newbury Park, CA: Sage.

Robinson, S. L., Kraatz, M. S. and Rousseau, D. M. (1994) Changing obligations and the psychological contract: a longitudinal study. *Academy of Management Journal*, **37**: 137–152.

Rousseau, D. M. & Wade-Benzoni, K. A. (1995) Changing individual–organization attachments: a two-way street. In A. Howard (Ed.), *The Changing Nature of Work*. San Francisco: Jossey-Bass.

Schein, E. H. (1978) *Career Dynamics: Matching Individual and Organizational Needs*. Reading, MA: Addison Wesley.

Smart, J. C., Elton, C. F. & McLaughlin, G. W. (1986) Person–environment congruence and job satisfaction. *Journal of Vocational Behavior*, **29**: 216–225.

Spokane, A. R. (1985). A review of research on person–environment congruence in Holland's theory of careers. *Journal of Vocational Behavior*, **26**: 306–343.

Sugalski, T. & Greenhaus, J. H. (1986) Career exploration and goal setting among managerial employees. *Journal of Vocational Behavior*, **29**: 102–114.

Super, D. E. (1980). A life-span, life-space approach to career development. *Journal of Vocational Behavior*, **16**: 282–298.

Waterman, R. H., Waterman, J. A. & Collard, B. A. (1994) Toward a career resilient workforce. *Harvard Business Review*, **July–August**: 87–95.

Weick, K. E. (1996) Enactment and the boundaryless career: organizing as we work. In M. Arthur & D. Rousseau (Eds), *The Boundaryless Career*. New York: Oxford University Press.

CHAPTER 6

# Work–Life Initiatives: Greed or Benevolence Regarding Workers' Time?

Catherine Kirchmeyer
*School of Business Administration, Wayne State University, USA*

## INTRODUCTION

Interest among both scholars and practitioners in the balance between workers' work and non-work domains surged during the 1980s and remains keen today. Agendas have broadened from mostly family-related issues, particularly for women, to quality-of-life and career issues for men and women. These trends are reflected in a recent shift in terminology, such as labeling work environments as "people-friendly" instead of "family-friendly" and organizational initiatives as "work–life" instead of "work–family". At the same time, employers have grown more cost-conscious, seeking tangible returns for work–life initiatives (Phillips 1997), and scholars more critical of the piecemeal approach of most initiatives (Parasuraman & Greenhaus 1997). Despite an ongoing diffusion of work–life initiatives throughout corporate America, employer involvement in workers' "private" lives has not gone unchallenged on economic and ethical grounds (Carlson 1993; Nash 1994).

Across the variety of opinions about employers' efforts to help workers balance life domains, the need to appreciate better the concept and the role of time is voiced consistently (e.g. Bailyn 1993; Brett 1997; Nash 1994; Raabe 1996). Common questions concern how hours of work relate to (and are perceived to relate to) job performance and organizational commitment, how time is (and should be) distributed between work and

*Trends in Organizational Behavior*, Volume 7. Edited by C. L. Cooper and D. M. Rousseau.
Copyright © 2000 John Wiley & Sons, Ltd.

non-work domains, and who should control this distribution. A fundamental question about the implications of work–life initiatives for workers' time, whether such implications are recognized by employers or not, also must be addressed. Are these initiatives the products of greedy organizations who wish to protect the workplace from the time demands of workers' non-work roles, or of benevolent organizations who wish to provide workers with the time to experience full lives?

Answering such questions concerning time is impeded by the lack of conceptual frameworks in this area that examine basic assumptions underlying work–life initiatives. The piecemeal approach of most initiatives is itself symptomatic of this conceptual deficiency. With many initiatives seemingly driven by pressures to comply with industrial and local trends (Goldstein 1994), organizational decision-makers have failed to develop genuine strategies with clear, consistent objectives to help workers' balance life domains. Strategy has been defined as a coherent, unifying, and integrative pattern of decisions (Hax & Majluf 1991), where objectives are determined, and action programs to achieve objectives are selected, from sets of alternatives. The act of strategic positioning forces decision-makers to identify key beliefs and convictions. Likewise, strategic positioning of work–life initiatives would involve the identification of basic assumptions about the work–non-work relationship, and the role of the employer in balancing life domains. It is upon such assumptions, once articulated, that a unifying strategy with consistent objectives can be built.

This chapter proposes a conceptual framework based on certain key assumptions to uncover the implications of work–life initiatives. The assumptions cover the distribution of responsibilities at work and outside of work, and the concepts of time and its control fall readily within this line of thinking. Such assumptions form the "conceptual core" of work–life initiatives, where the rationales that drive organizational action can be tapped, where fundamental questions about time can be addressed fully, and from which real change for workers can emerge. Honest inquiry at this level is recommended for organizational learning in general, although often it is difficult to achieve in work settings because of defensive behavior protecting the status quo (Argyris 1993).

The framework comprises a typology of organizational responses to non-work that is built on the work of several well-known scholars. First, in her seminal work on work and family, Kanter (1977) identified two distinct ways that employers have responded to family issues throughout the industrial age. The different assumptions underlying these responses about the work–family relationship became the foundation for the typology at hand. Secondly, Hall & Richter (1988) distinguished work–life initiatives in terms of their effects on the boundary between work and family. Their boundary dimensions, flexibility and permeability, were applied to the typology to determine the implications of employer responses for workers. Boundary flexibility refers to the extent that temporal and location markers between domains are moveable, whereas boundary permeability refers to the extent that the psychological concerns of one domain enter the physical location of the other. Finally, Coser's (1974) competing-roles theory was incorporated to identify the precise implications for time. In particular, his concept of greedy institutions served to explain why work–life initiatives do not necessarily help workers achieve balanced lives. The theories are clearly integrated in the discussion of the typology below.

A few words about "balanced lives" are necessary at this point. Those who write about work–life initiatives do not identify routinely what they mean by this term and rarely is a meaning sought. Yet, given its importance to understanding the management of life domains, and its openness to interpretation (see Primeau (1996) for full discussion), a meaning should be provided. In this chapter, a balanced life is identified as achieving satisfying experiences in all life domains, and to do so requires personal resources like energy, time, and commitment to be well distributed across domains. Balance allows one's various social roles to support and facilitate one another, rather than simply interfere with one another. This meaning is intended to reflect the common desire among people today to be accomplished in multiple life domains and the centrality of this multi-dimensionality to defining who they are (Robinson & Godbey 1997).

## ORGANIZATIONAL RESPONSES TO NON-WORK

### A Typology Based on Assumptions

This typology of organizational responses to non-work was developed initially to frame an empirical study (Kirchmeyer 1995), and is presented in Figure 6.1. Unlike the frameworks of others that distinguish responses by the extent of adaptation of work–life initiatives (Goldstein 1994; Ingram & Simons 1995), or by the stage of their evolution toward full integration with organizational culture (Galinsky, Friedman & Hernandez 1991), it is based on two sets of opposing assumptions. The assumptions address relationships between work and non-work domains and between employers and workers. Such assumptions are not necessarily acknowledged or espoused by organizational decision-makers, and are akin to Argyris' (1993) "theories in use" which actually are relied upon to design and carry out actions.

The horizontal dimension presents two opposing assumptions about the nature of the work–non-work relationship. One assumption holds

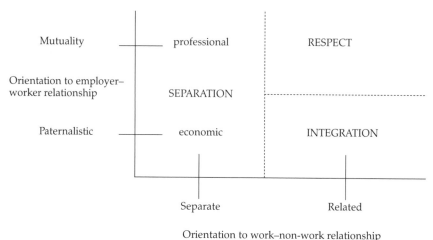

**Figure 6.1**  Typology of organizational responses

that work and non-work are separate worlds. From this position, employers are concerned mainly with workers fulfilling their work responsibilities and ignore other life domains. Workers' non-work responsibilities are considered to be solely the concern of workers themselves, and, in effect, workers are expected to leave their personal lives at the office or factory door. Separation of "official" and "personal" spheres of life represents a fundamental principle of the bureaucratic form of organization that has dominated this century (Weber 1947). Earlier forms such as those based on feudalism and craft guilds did not share this principle.

The opposing assumption holds that work and non-work are related worlds that affect one another. The attitudes and behavior of individuals at work are seen as products not only of the work environment, but of family and community experiences as well. Acknowledging such connectedness, employers cannot ignore workers' lives outside of work when establishing policies and practices and in day-to-day operations. Employers' interests clearly are served when workers' non-work roles do not impair their work capabilities. Therefore, it is from this position that employers accept responsibility for helping workers to balance work and non-work domains and work–life initiatives logically can arise.

The vertical dimension of the typology presents opposing assumptions about the nature of the employer–worker relationship. One position is called paternalism. Patriarchal refers to family and other social structures where power lies in the hands of the father or male elders. The central relationship is the father-dependent one (Morgan 1985). Employers with rational-legal authority, as opposed to patriarchal authority, that function in the manner of a father by usurping individual responsibility and freedom of choice are called paternalistic. Such employers are analogous to strict and controlling fathers and their workers to obedient and dependent children. Although paternalistic usually describes organizations that demonstrate a related orientation to the work–non-work relationship, its basic components of domination and unequal distribution of power can exist alongside a separate orientation. In this latter case, domination extends only to the work domain, and control and dependency issues remain largely economic in nature.

The opposing position assumes mutuality of the employer–worker relationship. Unlike paternalism that is analogous to a father-dependent relationship, mutuality involves a relationship between equals and is similar to the egalitarianism of modem family and other social structures. From this position, a better balance of power between workers and employers exists and reciprocity rather than domination serves as the motivating force. Workers enjoy considerable autonomy over their work and can be relied upon to abide by certain codes of conduct. Mutuality represents the traditional relationship with employers experienced by professional workers and is evident in "professional bureaucracies" such as hospitals, universities, and accounting firms. In his analysis of organizational forms, Mintzberg (1981) found the professional bureaucracy to be the most democratic of all, with much operating and strategic decision-making lying in the hands of professionals.

Although the two dimensions of assumptions create four quadrants, only three response-types are implied by the logic. That is, assuming work and non-work to be separate worlds means disregard for workers' outside lives, and no work–life initiative, regardless of which assumption about the employer–worker relationship is held. However, once non-work is assumed to affect work, the response-type becomes dependent on how the employer–worker relationship is viewed. The implications of the three response-types for workers' time are developed in respective sections below and summarized in Figure 6.2.

Because most work–life initiatives today follow a piecemeal or practice-by-practice approach, the response-types must be considered abstract or "ideal" (Weber 1947), that is, normative and pure in theory. The initiatives of any one employer might be drawn from all types in reality. Nonetheless, the typology provides a way to make distinctions among the array of practices, including their implications for workers' time. The ordering of the types below follows the assumptions across the dimensions and is not chronological or reflective of prevalence. The typical response-type of employers has shifted over time as a result of political, economic, and social factors. As Morgan & Tucker (1991) point out in

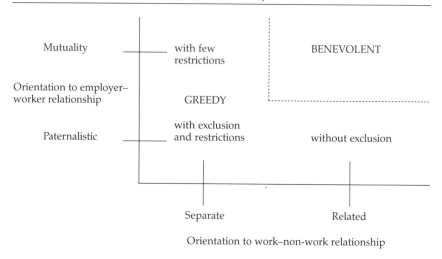

**Figure 6.2**    Implications for workers' time

their historical overview, employer interest in workers' non-work lives is almost as old as the industrial revolution and work–life initiatives should not be considered a modern phenomenon. This point also is developed further below.

*Separation Response*

The separation response is based on the assumption of work and non-work being separate worlds and occupies the left-hand side of the typology in Figure 6.1. In this case, the employer plays no role in helping workers' balance their lives. Kanter (1977) provided a lengthy discussion of the prevalence of separation throughout the twentieth century. In terms of Hall & Richter's (1988) boundary concepts, separation supports high inflexibility of the work–non-work boundary with temporal markers between work and non-work remaining firm. That is, work begins and ends at precise, predetermined times regardless of workers' personal needs.

Employers, however, are more accepting of work demands, as compared to non-work demands, shifting temporal markers, such as workers staying beyond normal work hours during busy periods, and pressures for them to do so depend on the nature of the employer–worker relationship. Although separation implies boundary impermeability as well as inflexibility, its total disregard of non-work concerns may lead to psychological disruption across domains. For example, a worker away on vacation becomes concerned with work when he or she receives a telephone call from a boss who is disrespectful of workers' personal lives, and in another instance, a worker becomes preoccupied with the family during the work day when a family matter must be left unresolved in the morning.

According to Coser's (1974) competing-roles theory, employers who set rigid boundaries to guard work against the time demands of other domains demonstrate greed for workers' time. He argued that fragmentation of commitment across domains characterizes modern social life, and "various groups having a claim on individuals' energies and time compete with one another in an effort to draw as much as they can" (p. 1). Such tensions, he believed, are not especially damaging to individuals as long as all of the claimants control only one life domain and are subject to normative and/or legal restrictions. In other words, when their control extends only to work and is subject to government regulations and cultural norms governing hours of work, greedy employers need not prevent workers from experiencing balanced lives.

The principles of bureaucracy include both the separation of official and private spheres of life and the rigidification of temporal boundaries (Zerubavel 1981). Weber (1947) argued a century ago that these principles contribute to making bureaucracy the most efficient means for large-scale administration, and support for them is not antiquated. Nash (1994), a critic of today's work–life trends across corporate America, advocates that employers serve workers best when they stay out of workers' private lives, reward them with good paychecks instead of with fringe benefits, which some workers may not value or utilize, and set sensible limits to the hours of work. Adherence to bureaucratic principles concerning work–non-work separation remains typical of employers today in other countries. Freese (2000), for example, reported such adherence for employers in The Netherlands. Interestingly, bureaucracy has its roots in Europe where it emerged after the breakdown of more traditional forms of authority and was favored for its social leveling influence (Weber 1947). Over the same period, the provision of family benefits largely became the responsibility of European governments as opposed to employers.

Although disregard of workers' outside lives indicates a separation response to non-work regardless of the employer–worker relationship, the implications for workers' time when relationships are based on paternalism differ somewhat from those when relationships are based on mutuality. In the case of paternalism when domination extends only to the work domain, control and dependency issues remain largely economic in nature. Time has economic value and represents both a commodity for exchange and a mechanism of control. Employers, in effect, buy workers' time, and like other scarce resources, time must be managed well to maximize corporate efficiency. Workers having discretion over the use of time is incompatible with paternalism, where control is the prerogative of the father-like employers. The bureaucratic principles stipulating separation of private and public spheres, and rigid temporal boundaries, however, fall within the logic of this relationship, and workers' non-work domains receive protection from the intrusions of work (Zerubavel 1981). The shifting of temporal markers by work demands evokes an economic exchange and quite simply demanding more time from workers can be costly to employers.

In contrast, when the employer–worker relationship is based on mutuality, the inaccessibility of workers' non-work domains by work dissolves. As Zerubavel (1981) argued in her analysis of private versus public time, the private time of low-status workers is more protected than that of high-status ones like professionals. Hence, having more freedom at work does not necessarily mean that workers experience greater balance to their lives. To understand why flexibility and autonomy can become burdens, the traditional conception of the professional role must be appreciated. Professionals, for example, are expected to be highly committed to their work, such that work takes precedence over all other aspects of life (Bailyn 1993). They typically are inseparable from their occupational roles, and, thus, always accessible. Zerubavel (1981) used physicians who pledged to "be ever ready to obey the calls of the sick" to demonstrate constant availability. Other examples include ministers and rabbis for whom living "one's work is a sign of holiness and calling" (Marciano 1990, p. 172), and even college professors, especially now with communication technologies allowing students remote accessibility to them. Zerubavel argued that constant availability is a symbolic expression of professional dedication, and indirectly of high status, and can explain the rise of the beeper as a modern status symbol. Relationships between professionals and their employers are not simply economic in nature, but involve exchanges of commitment for status, autonomy, and other privileges as well. In addition, due to the difficulties of measuring performance in some professions, visible time on-the-job may serve as a barometer of professional productivity for employers.

Hence, boundary flexibility and boundary permeability appear to be inherent to the professional role, and given the demands for high work commitment, work typically invades the space of non-work, rather than non-work invading work space. Bailyn's (1993) account of the effects of the professorial role on private life provides an insightful example of the engaging quality of academic work, and how flexibility combined with unbounded work expectations can rob professors of the time to experience balanced lives. In terms of Coser's (1974) theory, greedy employers represent a threat to professionals because their claims for time are subject to few legal or cultural restrictions.

The resource demands of the traditional professional role also apply to a new breed of "professionalized" workers when employers disregard their private lives. These workers do not belong to the traditional professions defined by the standardization of skills and outside accreditation (Mintzberg 1981), but adopt a professional ideology in exchange for professional privileges. They demonstrate strong commitment to their work and are entrusted with considerable autonomy. Often they are paid by salary, the same amount regardless of how many hours are worked, and their private lives are accessible to work demands. In her report of this occupational trend, Schor (1991) described how corporate values that emphasize commitment, initiative, and flexibility often translate into constant availability for workers. The remarks of one executive capture this predicament well. "People who work for me should have phones in their bathrooms" (p. 19).

*Integration Response*

A second type of organizational response to non-work has been prevalent throughout the industrial age as well (Kanter 1977). It occupies the lower right-hand corner of the typology in Figure 6.1. In this case, employers view work and non-work as related worlds that affect one another and act to integrate them in an effort to reduce inter-domain conflict. Hence, the response is called integration. Typically, it has involved employers assuming responsibility for aspects of workers' personal lives. In their historical account of work and family, Morgan & Tucker (1991) described an array of integration practices including employer-supported childcare centers, company schools and recreation facilities, take-home meals, and medical services. They remarked how many ideas and models established almost 200 years ago resemble current ones. In an assessment of modern work–life initiatives, Hall & Richter (1988) concluded that many of them entail greater integration of work and non-work domains. Among the most prevalent examples are employee assistance programs, childcare centers, work–family seminars, and spousal employment assistance (Freidman & Johnson 1997).

The idea of employers assuming responsibility for aspects of workers' private lives, and in a sense "taking control" fits a paternalistic model of the employer–worker relationship. The worker is analogous to the dependent child receiving the protection of, and other benefits from, the more powerful father. Extreme examples of the integration response and its paternalistic nature were seen in some early American corporations where workplaces became "total institutions" in the form of company towns providing for workers' family, community, and recreation needs (Kanter 1977).

The early efforts of employers to integrate work and non-work were motivated primarily by the need for educated, obedient, and loyal workers. Morgan & Tucker (1991) reported that proponents of employer-sponsored schools and preschools of the nineteenth century emphasized the reduction of stress and worry so parents could concentrate on work. Likewise, modern work–life initiatives often are intended to enable mothers to work (Lewis 1996) and workers with family responsibilities more easily to spend time and energy at work (Bailyn 1993). Benefits that reduce workers' work–non-work conflict, however, do not necessarily help them achieve more balanced lives. For example, a worker with heavy work demands may experience little work–non-work conflict as long as non-work demands are few, but his or her life probably would not be described as balanced. With integration, workers resources are not better distributed across domains and they do not gain the time to attend to non-work roles. In addition, Hall & Richter (1988) argued that integration blurs distinctions of roles and activities outside of work with those of work, resulting in high permeability of the work–non-work boundary.

Hence, adopting the position of work and non-work being related worlds fails to deter employers' greed for workers' time and may even intensify it. According to Coser's (1974) reasoning, once employers extend their control beyond the work domain, they grow more threatening to workers. Without competing claimants for workers' energies and time, the potential for extreme control and dependency exists. In terms of the patriarchal analogy, the child risks becoming entirely dependent on an over-controlling father. Ford's US$5 per day workers who were subjected to home visits by "social investigators" to ensure their characters and families met company standards (Carlson 1993) come to mind. Employer–worker relationships involving exchanges of loyalty for protection may have been appropriate when workers remained with the same employers for a lifetime, but they seem inconsistent with the uncertainties of employment today. Nash (1994), for example, asked, if a person's "entire health-support and child-support system is sponsored by the corporation, what happens should he be laid off?" (p. 21). The personal consequences from being laid off may be especially damaging psychologically as well as economically if workers' social networks and support systems are derived exclusively from the work domain.

*Respect Response*

So far, most organizational efforts to help workers balance their life domains have been consistent with an integration response to non-work. Critical thinkers, however, suggest that another type of response fits better with current employment and social realities and also supports work–

life initiatives. For example, they advocate "partnerships" between employers and workers (Friedman, Christensen & Degroot 1998; Orthner, Bowen & Beare 1990), "shared responsibility" (Bankert & Lobel 1997), and conditions of "mutual flexibility" (Gonyea & Googins 1996). Underlying this alternative way of thinking is an employer–worker relationship based on mutuality where both parties are equally dependent on one another for consideration and support in order to succeed.

On the typology in Figure 6.1, the third type of organizational response to non-work rests in the upper right-hand corner and is called respect. Respect refers to the employer acknowledging and valuing the private lives of workers, and committing to support them. The worker, however, is considered independent and capable of self-determination and no longer analogous to a dependent child. Employers do not aim to take over workers' non-work responsibilities, but rather, to provide workers with the personal resources to fulfill such responsibilities themselves. In effect, the autonomy that traditional professionals experienced over work now extends to non-work domains. Moreover, with respect, employers and workers can achieve genuine reciprocity involving complex series of exchanges across the parties. Friedman, Christensen & DeGroot (1998), for example, refer to a "virtuous cycle", where employers provide workers with resources to manage their lives, workers feel stronger commitment to the organization, trust and loyalty levels increase, workers invest more energy at work, personal productivity improves, and ultimately organizational performance is enhanced.

To implement the respect response, Hall & Richter (1988) suggest that boundary flexibility represents the key. That is, temporal and location markers with work become moveable and responsive to both work and non-work demands. At the same time, boundaries remain impermeable to psychological crossover; an important distinction from the constant availability experienced by traditional professionals. Likewise, Friedman, Christensen and DeGroot (1998) recommend the establishment of "effective" boundaries between domains to "remove distractions, allowing people to be more fully focused on the task at hand" (p. 122). Thus, with respect, rather than integrating work and non-work domains and closing the gap between them, the gap actually is maintained. Common examples of work–life initiatives consistent with respect include flexible hours of work, alternative work sites, and policies that discourage work-related travel on weekends.

Because work–life initiatives based on respect do not focus on guarding work against the resource demands of workers' other domains, they fail to demonstrate the greed for workers' energies and time described by Coser (1974). Respect represents the only response-type of the typology where workers gain time to attend to non-work roles and employers can be considered benevolent. By supporting the resource needs of workers' personal lives, employers demonstrate a more collaborative, and less competing, approach to the distribution of workers' time. Full collaboration demands a recognition by employers that workers' involvement in non-work domains enhances their work capabilities, and thereby, contributes to organizational functioning. Thus, employers' benevolence concerning time serves themselves as well as workers and seems economically and ethnically astute.

Linking workers' needs and business goals to create "win–win" situations represents the central theme of two recent articles on work–life initiatives in high-profile, business publications (Bailyn, Fletcher & Kolb 1997; Friedman, Christensen & DeGroot 1998). The articles provide rich examples of the respect response in action that demonstrate well the strong commitment and vigilance required to make it succeed. Relationships based on mutuality, whether in the family, work setting, or elsewhere, demand openness, trust, and constant updating and discussion of the parties' goals and priorities to flourish. Meeting these demands may represent large hurdles for both employers and workers. Some scholars (e.g. Brett 1997; Haas & Hwang 1995) remain skeptical about their willingness and ability to do so at this time given that the required attitudes and behavior often are inconsistent with organizational cultures and even society at large.

## CONCLUSIONS

Balancing life domains remains a top priority among North American workers today (Friedman & Johnson 1997). Employers, whether or not they are motivated merely by competitive pressures, probably will continue to respond to this reality with work–life initiatives. To move these initiatives to a strategic level where consistent objectives can be set, organizational decision-makers must examine their basic assumptions or theories in use. As demonstrated in this chapter, opposing sets of assumptions about the work–non-work relationship and about the employer–worker relationship provide a framework for such an examination and paired together they reveal distinct types of organizational responses to non-work. At this conceptual core, the time implications of each response-type are readily uncovered. Particularly revealing is that work–life initiatives do not necessarily help workers experience more balanced lives. This is so because initiatives do not always result in a better distribution of personal resources across life domains.

The implications of each response-type for workers' time are summarized in Figure 6.2. Greed for workers' time dominates much of the typology. That is, in three of the four quadrants, employers compete for workers' energies and time and aim to draw as much as they can. Greedy employers, however, need not prevent workers from experiencing balanced lives as long as their control extends only to work and is subject to normative and/or legal restrictions. With an integration response, the control of greedy employers is not exclusive to work. Thus, integration represents a greater threat to workers achieving balance than a separation response with strict adherence to bureaucratic principles. This conclusion does not infer that initiatives arising from integration, such as employee assistance programs and childcare centers, have no merit. Clearly they do. They simply do not provide workers with more personal resources. Employers that grant worker's autonomy over work while expecting constant availability also demonstrate greed for workers' time and are especially threatening because their greed has few restrictions. It is only with a respect response, where employers demonstrate a collaborative approach to the distribution of workers' personal resources, that they can be considered benevolent regarding workers' time. With a better distribution of resources across domains, workers can experience more balanced lives.

Although the typology of organizational responses to non-work is based on observations of the American corporate setting, it has application beyond this one location. In fact, it may prove helpful for distinguishing the predominant types of responses across countries, and provide a conceptual tool for cross-cultural analyses. For example, comparisons of the responses of American employers to non-work with those of European employers are often undertaken (e.g. Bailyn 1993; Lewis 1997; Schor 1991). The common impression is that Europeans are granted more time by employers to attend to non-work roles and experience more balanced lives. However, are European employers really more benevolent than American ones concerning workers' time or is their greed simply more restricted by state legislation? Answering this question through careful analysis is beyond the scope of this chapter. It is posed merely as an example of the application possibilities of the conceptual framework presented here.

The process of organizational decision-makers and scholars examining the basic assumptions underlying work–life initiatives is consistent with the change efforts advocated by others in the literature (e.g. Bailyn 1993; Friedman & Johnson 1997; Lewis 1996). They argue that to really change workers' lives, work–life initiatives must be part of a culture change in the organization itself. Culture change involves exposing, challenging, and altering the predominant theories in use. Without a firm grasp of the thinking that drives organizational action, the implications of any change effort will remain elusive and its ability to achieve consistent outcomes unlikely. Employers and workers often feel uncomfortable tackling this conceptual core. It can be mentally and emotionally demanding work that the hectic pace of organizational life, and emotions like fear and distrust, discourage. The typology in this chapter presents them with a practical tool for focusing their thinking.

Finally, the typology of organizational responses to non-work provides a conceptual framework for researchers to develop and test hypotheses concerning the outcomes of work–life initiatives beyond time-related ones. Earlier frameworks based on the extent or stage of initiative implementation seem inappropriate for identifying commonalities and distinctions among the array of practices. One empirical study that applied the typology (Kirchmeyer 1995) provided evidence of the response-types having distinct effects on work attitudes and spill-over between work and non-work. Understanding the particular outcomes that can be expected from work–life initiatives would help employers to set clear objectives and move their initiatives to a truly strategic level.

## REFERENCES

Argyris, C. (1993) *Knowledge for Action*. San Francisco: Jossey-Bass.

Bailyn, L. (1993) *Breaking the Mold*. New York: The Free Press.

Bailyn, L., Fletcher, J. K. & Kolb, D. (1997) Unexpected connections: considering employees' personal lives can revitalize your business. *Sloan Management Review*, **Summer**: 11–19.

Bankert, E. C. & Lobel, S. A. (1997) Visioning the future. In S. Parasuraman & J. H. Greenhaus (Eds), *Integrating Work And Family* (pp. 177–191). Westport, CT: Quorum.

Brett, J. M. (1997) Family, sex, and career advancement. In S. Parasuraman & J. H. Greenhaus (Eds), *Integrating Work and Family* (pp. 143–153). Westport, CT: Quorum.

Carlson, A. C. (1993) *From Cottage to Work Station*. San Francisco: Ignatius Press.

Coser, L. A. (1974) *Greedy Institutions*. New York: The Free Press.

Freese, C. (2000). Psychological contracts in the Netherlands. In D. M. Rousseau & R. Schalk (Eds), *Psychological Contracts in Employment*. Newbury Park, CA: Sage.

Friedman, D. E. & Johnson, A. A. (1997) Moving from programs to culture change: the next stage for the corporate work–family agenda. In S. Parasuraman & J. H. Greenhaus (Eds), *Integrating Work and Family* (pp. 192–208). Westport, CT: Quorum.

Friedman, S. D., Christensen, P. & DeGroot, J. (1998) Work and life: the end of the zero-sum game. *Harvard Business Review*, **76**: 119–129.

Galinsky, E., Friedman, D. E. & Hernandez, C. A. (1991) *The Corporate Reference Guide to Work–Family Programs*. New York: Families and Work Institute.

Goldstein, J. D. (1994) Institutional pressures and strategic-responsiveness: employer involvement in work–family issues. *Academy of Management Journal*, **37**: 350–382.

Gonyea, J. G. & Googins, B. (1996) The restructuring of work and family in the United States: a new challenge for American corporations. In S. Lewis & J. Lewis (Eds), *The Work–Family Challenge*, (pp. 63–78). Thousand Oaks, CA: Sage.

Haas, L. & Hwang, P. (1995) Company culture and men's usage of family leave benefits in Sweden. Family *Relations*, **44**: 28–36.

Hall, D. T. & Richter, J. (1988) Balancing work life and home life: what can organizations do to help? *Academy of Management Executive*, **2**: 213–223.

Hax, A. C. & Majluf, N. S. (1991) *The Strategy Concept and Process*. Englewood Cliffs, NJ: Prentice-Hall.

Ingram, P. & Simons, T. (1995) Institutional and resource dependence determinants of responsiveness to work–family issues. *Academy of Management Journal*, **38**: 1466–1482.

Kanter, R. M. (1977) *Work and Family in the United States: A Critical Review and Agenda for Research and Policy*. New York: Russell Sage Foundation.

Kirchmeyer, C. (1995) Managing the work–non-work boundary: an assessment of organizational responses. *Human Relations*, **48**: 515–536.

Lewis, S. (1996) Rethinking employment: an organizational culture change framework. In S. Lewis & J. Lewis (Eds), *The Work–Family Challenge* (pp. 1–19). Thousand Oaks, CA: Sage.

Lewis, S. (1997) An international perspective on work–family issues. In S. Parasuraman & J. H. Greenhaus (Eds), *Integrating Work and Family*, (pp. 91–103). Westport, CT: Quorum.

Marciano, T. D. (1990) Corporate church, ministry, and ministerial family: embedded employment and measures of success. In R. S. Hanks & M. B. Sussman (Eds), *Corporations, Businesses, and Families*, (pp. 171–193). New York: The Haworth Press.

Mintzberg, H. (1981) Organization design: fashion or fit? *Harvard Business Review*, **59**: 103–116.

Morgan, D. H. J. (1985) *The Family, Politics and Social Theory*. London: Routledge & Kegan Paul.

Morgan, H. & Tucker, K. (1991) *Companies That Care*. New York: Simon & Schuster.

Nash. L. L. (1994) The Nanny Corporation. *Across The Board*, **July/August**: 16–22.

Orthner, D. K., Bowen, G. L. & Beare, V. G. (1990) The organization family: a question of work and family boundaries. In R. S. Hanks & M. B. Sussman (Eds), *Corporations, Businesses and Families* (pp. 15–36). New York: The Haworth Press.

Parasuraman, S. & Greenhaus, J. H. (1997) Issues and challenges in managing work–family linkages. In S. Parasuraman & J. H. Greenhaus (Eds), *Integrating Work and Family* (pp. 3–14). Westport, CT: Quorum.

Phillips, T. (1997). The work–family issue from a consultant's perspective. In S. Parasuraman & J. H. Greenhaus (Eds), *Integrating Work and Family* (pp. 38–47). Westport, CT: Quorum.

Primeau, L. A. (1996) Work and leisure: transcending the dichotomy. *The American Journal of Occupational Therapy*, **50**: 569–577.

Raabe, P. H. (1996) Constructing pluralistic work and career arrangements. In S. Lewis & J. Lewis (Eds), *The Work–Family Challenge* (pp. 128–141). Thousand Oaks, CA: Sage.

Robinson, J. P. & Godbey, G. (1997) *Time for Life*. University Park, PA: Pennsylvania State University Press.

Schor, J. B. (1991) *The Overworked American*. New York: Basic Books.

Weber, M. (1947) *The Theory of Social and Economic Organization*. London: Free Press.

Zerubavel, E. (1981) *Hidden Rhythms*. Chicago, IL: The University of Chicago Press.

# CHAPTER 7

# Organizational Identity in Transition over Time

Kevin G. Corley and Dennis A. Gioia
*Penn State University, USA*

and

Tommaso Fabbri
*University of Modena, Italy*

## INTRODUCTION

*Everything changes and nothing changes.*

This bit of philosophical wisdom, which has shown up in many different incarnations in many different traditions of humanist study, is usually treated by academic scholars either as opaque doublespeak or as some sort of impenetrable paradox. Organization study has largely ignored this sort of paradox, usually choosing to observe that at times things change and at other times things stay the same—a kind of punctuated equilibrium approach to paradox.

Ironically, it is in the study of change itself that this little semantic dance gets played out most obviously. Our literature, perhaps especially in the writings of the late 1990s, is inclined to argue that organizations *must* change and change quickly. Time horizons are foreshortening. No change, slow change, and in the case of the more strident voices, even moderately paced change, in the face of quickly changing environments is seen as a virtual passport to a passé organization. On the other hand, this stance implies the fulfillment of Toffler's (1970) thesis that the pace of

*Trends in Organizational Behavior*, Volume 7. Edited by C. L. Cooper and D. M. Rousseau.

change would soon exceed the human capacity to cope with it—a state that some would argue we have now achieved in many organizations, coincident with the turn of the millennium. Therefore, a counter-stance has arisen that people need stability in organizational life to avoid producing manic, information-overloaded, unfocused activity. The unsatisfying resolution to the paradox thus takes the following form: yes, some things (e.g. technological capability) must change, but other things (core values, needs) do not change (Collins & Porras 1994). Or, as President Jimmy Carter declared at his inaugural, "We must adjust to changing times and still hold to unchanging principles" (20 January 1977).

The one hot area of study that sometimes seems to be trying to stay above this fray is the study of organizational identity. Concern with organizational identity has been around for a long time, but only under the label of *identity* since Albert & Whetten's (1985) treatise. These authors held strongly that organizational identity should be defined and treated as those features of an organization that were central, distinctive, and enduring—i.e. core sets of beliefs that distinguished the organization from others and which did not change over time. Even during the middle 1990s heyday of heated discussions about the need for organizations to change in response to, among other things, *hyper*competition (D'Aveni 1994), Whetten (1995) continued to argue provocatively that, "If it isn't core, enduring, and distinctive, it isn't identity." For organizational identity, then, time would seem to stand still, somehow immune from the fads, folderol, and alleged superficialities of a media-driven era that insists that *everything* must change.

We have thus arrived breathless and hyperventilating at the turn of the millennium, assuming that almost everything about organizations is changing, with the one possible exception of the safe haven of identity. Yet, how do we reconcile this notion of stability in identity with another new-age bit of (ancient) wisdom, "that everything changes and nothing abides" (cf. Heraclitus via Plato, 402 B.C.)? Gioia & Thomas (1996) argued that we cannot even talk about bona fide organizational change (transformational change according to Jick's (1992) typology) unless we recognize that some core features of organizations; namely, facets of identity, are changing. And, if some core facets are changing, can we then say that identity itself is changing? We face a conceptual conundrum about a concept of central concern in a year of symbolic significance. Is identity an exemplar of stability that does not change in a sea of change? Or, is it yet another pretender that changes like everything else, despite the possibility that advocates for its stability might be in denial about its alleged immutability? Or, is it perhaps an ideal exemplar of the introductory paradox that, where identity is concerned, things change and things stay the same?

## IDENTITY, TIME AND CHANGE

The theme of this book is time and, by implication, change over time. As is evident from the above discussion, we believe that identity (perhaps especially at the organization level, but also at the individual level) provides a fitting context for discussing notions of time, change, and stability in modern organizations. Identity is usually taken to be essentially immutable; yet, as with all things in our media-driven, internet-connected world, we will argue that identity cannot help but change. Change in identity does not require a formal effort from the top of an organization or even a ground-swell of support from lower levels (although we do not deny that such change occurs), but can transpire simply with the passing of time and shifting of member perceptions. Such change, even if the change is not evident or is denied, can afford individuals and organizations the flexibility and adaptability necessary for survival and growth (Gioia, Schultz & Corley, 2000).

From this standpoint, the important question is not, "Does identity change?", but rather, "Over what period of time does identity change?" The deceptively apparent answer is, "over long periods of time", because otherwise, how else could we be said to be working for the same organization day after day, month after month? We argue in this chapter, however, that identity actually adapts over surprisingly short periods of time as other processes work simultaneously to facilitate and to disguise changes in identity, even to those individuals laboring to construct identity as stable. Before exploring this argument, we first render a brief, selective overview of the main works that have led us to this point and our concern with time and change.

## A WHIRLWIND TOUR OF IDENTITY THEORY AND RESEARCH

Identity at the organization level refers to self-reflective questions by organization members such as, "Who are we as an organization?" or, "What do we want to be as an organization?" In their influential work originally defining the concept, Albert & Whetten (1985) conceptualized organizational identity as those features of an organization collectively understood by its members to be *central*, *distinctive*, and *enduring*, This definition was meant to provide a way for researchers and organization members alike to characterize and distinguish an organization based upon those aspects perceived to be most important by insiders. These defining aspects were conceived as stable and resistant to ephemeral or faddish attempts at alteration because of their ties to the organization's founding and history. Although Albert & Whetten acknowledged that identity could change, they argued that change only occurred slowly, over long periods of time.

It was some time, however, before the conceptualization was picked up and used empirically to any major extent. Dutton & Dukerich's (1991) examination of the New York/New Jersey Port Authority and its attempts to adapt to environmental changes provided an initial, empirically grounded look at how identity interacts with individual-level variables to help influence organizational sensemaking and behavior. Their analysis revealed a rather close relationship between members' sense of organizational self and appropriate ways of interpreting and reacting to feedback from outsiders regarding the organization and its previous actions. Additionally, they introduced the notion of image (a term they later renamed "construed external image"—Dutton, Dukerich & Harquail 1994) to explain how members' sense of outsiders' perceptions of the organization interacted with identity to augment the links between individual cognition and behavior and subsequent organizational action.

Furthering the notion of a relationship between identity and image, Whetten, Lewis & Mischel (1992) introduced the notion of an identity congruence as those occurrences where insider perceptions of the organization matched with the images projected by the organization (a definition of image that implied more interdependence with external influences than Dutton & Dukerich's (1991), conceptualization) and with how outsiders perceived the organization. This trifecta of perceptual alignments was posited to afford the organization increased ability to adapt to changes in the internal and external environments.

Dutton, Dukerich & Harquail (1994) were also concerned with the alignment between internal and external perceptions of the organization in their theoretical examination of the impact various organizational images might have on member identification. Building a strong theoretical link between (individual-level) social identity theory (Ashforth & Mael 1989; Tajfel & Turner 1985), organizational identity, and organizational image, Dutton and her colleagues were able to provide a solid foundation from which future researches could empirically investigate relations between individuals and their organizations.

Elsbach & Kramer's (1996) examination of how members of top 20 business schools responded to reputational rankings provided an excellent example of empirical research based on these previous efforts. Hypothesizing a strong link between organizational and social identities, Elsbach & Kramer used the threats to identity present in reputational rankings as an opportunity to explore how organization members responded to feedback about their organizations that differed from their own perceptions. Their findings that insiders re-framed the organization's identity based on the perceived level of dissonance between the identity and the reputational feedback (similar to James' (1918), looking-glass self) demonstrated the powerful influence of outsiders' perceptions on organizational identity.

An additional line of inquiry, less concerned with individual-level outcomes and more interested in organization-level outcomes, involved the relationship between organizational identity and organizational change. In a detailed analysis of the theoretical aspects of implementing a total quality initiative, Reger *et al.* (1994) argued that such a fundamental change in the way an organization conducted its business required a fundamental change in how the organization thought of itself. Only by bringing about changes in the organization's identity could a top management team successfully implement the often radical transformations that Total Quality Management initiatives required.

Their theorizing on the relationship between organizational identity and change found support in Gioia & Thomas's (1996) empirical examination of a strategic change effort at a large public research university. Beyond finding general support for a relationship between identity and change, Gioia & Thomas found that it was the link between identity and projected image, specifically a desired future image projected by the top management team, that formed the conceptual foundation of strategic change within the university. By presenting an alternative perspective as to what the organization could be, the top management team was able to bring about changes in the organization's identity and create support for the changes desired in the change effort. This study also provided the first empirical evidence that identity was not (and probably could not be) as stable as previously theorized. Their findings indicated that the university's identity was not only capable of relatively rapid change, but that it was malleable in its ability to adapt to environmental changes.

Both lines of inquiry came together in a series of conferences held in 1994, 1995, and 1996 dedicated to the topic of identity in organizations. These meetings afforded a diverse groups of researchers the chance to interact and share ideas on the identity of organizations, the identity of people within organizations, as well as people's identification with organizations. The ultimate outcome of these conferences was a volume (Whetten & Godfrey 1998) documenting a number of the conversations that took place on a wide range of theoretical and empirical topics concerning identity. These conversations, along with the articles in the Special Topic Forum on Identity and Identification published in the *Academy of Management Review* in 2000, provided an effective capstone to theory and research on identity in organizations during the twentieth century.

In this forum, Gioia, Shultz & Corley (2000) expanded on the findings from Gioia & Thomas's (1996) research in explaining why identity should be conceptualized as fluid and malleable because of its interrelationships with image. These relationships provide organizations with an "adaptive instability" in their dealings with changing and fragmented environments. In a related vein, Pratt & Foreman (2000) provided a detailed review of work on the concept of multiple identities within organizations and suggestions for how future research should proceed in examining this phenomenon. Scott & Lane (2000) took a stakeholder approach and examined how the relationship between managers and stakeholders provides an organization with the ability to manage its organizational identity and the identifications of its members. All in all, the study of organizational identity has become quite a focal topic as we move into the twenty-first century.

## THE SEDUCTIVENESS OF MICRO–MACRO PARALLELS IN IDENTITY

Identity is a captivating concept in part because of the parallels between individual identity and organizational identity; the concept resonates at both the micro and macro levels. Just as having a sense of individual self is important, having a sense of collective self is also important when that collective becomes part of the individual's self-definition. However, just because identity is as important at one level as it is at the next does not mean that identity should be conceptualized identically at both levels. Even though extensions of individual identity notions have greatly influenced conceptions of organizational identity, such that our taken-for-granted assumptions regarding the stability of organizational identity mirror those of the (apparent) stability at the individual level, it is essential to recognize that there are differences in the ways in which identity should be viewed at each level (Rousseau 1985). Considering those differences can help relate the two concepts together to form a bigger picture of individual–organization interaction and the susceptibility of identity to change.

Gioia (1998) has argued that there are a number of important ways in which organizational identity can be seen as similar to, but different from, individual identity. First, organizations can more easily be viewed as harboring multiple identities (Pratt & Foreman 2000), each tailored to the differing contexts with which the organization must deal. This can be seen as arising out of the principle of requisite variety, wherein a system should attempt to approximate the complexity of the environment it faces. Take, for instance, the modern research university and the multiplicity of identities co-existing within its permeable boundaries—with stakeholders ranging from parents of high school students to professors to alumni to corporate partners to various levels of government. The notion of a single, unifying identity almost seems laughable in the face of such diffusion and complexity. An individual displaying the multiple identities that are taken for granted at the organizational level would be deemed dysfunctionally schizophrenic, yet this characteristic is necessary and easily enacted for organizations.

Furthermore, an organization can, and often must, enact such multiple identities *simultaneously* as it interacts with different constituencies. Again, because of the diverse expectations placed on it by various aspects of the environment, the research university must be both traditional and cutting-edge concurrently as it strives to maintain its legitimacy as a haven of personal growth and education while fostering a reputation for innovation and development (and thus as a good investment for corporate partners and alumni). These related features also suggest a facile capability for organizations to shift among identities as the context demands, while nonetheless appearing to be internally consistent.

Secondly, virtually all views, regardless of level of analysis, conceive of identity as a self-concept formed and sustained by social interaction. The implications of this observation for organizational identity are more profound than for individual identity. Modern organizational environments change rapidly. Contextual and competitive features (the "social" interaction of organizations) change frequently, implying accelerated changes in structures, processes, products, and services—which, in turn, imply changes in the features that help to define the identity of the organization and suggest relatively rapid reconstructions of identity. Environmental changes influence identity changes; if environments change quickly, then identity becomes vulnerable to change.

## THE MALLEABILITY OF INDIVIDUAL IDENTITY

It is interesting to ask if some of these observations made in trying to discern the nature of organizational identity might not also have implications for (re)conceptualizing individual identity. Certainly, we can note that one of the most common orientations in the field of psychology since its inception has been to characterize individuals in terms of stable qualities that remain invariant across situations, whether these qualities are located in stable individual dispositions or stable patterns of behavior (Mischel & Shoda 1995). Most notably, individual identity has been presumed to be *the* invariant individual difference feature. As it turns out, however, despite this widespread lay and professional presumption, there is ample evidence of thinking that characterizes individual identity as rather fluid. Recent treatises in psychology acknowledge and explore the malleability of identity (Markus & Nurius 1986; Scheibe 1995). Much of this alternative thinking, though, is more richly expressed in works deriving from philosophy and the humanities. It is intriguing to very briefly consider the tenor of some of this work in understanding the changeable character of individual identity.

Perhaps not unexpectedly, time is heavily implicated in discussions of fluid identity. Luhmann (1990) notes that the construction of the temporal dimension depends on the possibility of simultaneously observing movement and stillness. We can see events and change only if something in the background stays still; and we can see stability only if there are changes in the background. So, depending on what we keep in the background, we can describe or represent what we see in two different ways. One is duration, from which we can remember the past or imagine the future (i.e. as structure); the other is flow—a sequence of events and transformations (i.e. as process). We should also note that both can occur together, thus giving us another basis for the observation that nothing changes and everything changes. For Luhmann, identity is not what is enduring and distinctive, but rather what one currently thinks to be enduring and distinctive of him- or herself. Identity becomes unchangeable only if it evolves into some permanent structure of expectancies, which is rare. According to Luhmann, the apparent stability of identity does not stem from some inner, invariable core, but from the attempt to maintain the ordering of social experience (which is itself actually changing).

Foucault (1988) (as referenced in Martin, Gutman, & Hutton 1988) also holds that identity is a subjectively variable personal construction. We self-select a set of definitions from among the many continuously generated in our everyday social reality. Importantly for Foucault, identity is not held in memory, but in the repetition of selected definitions—in repeated application of some self-representation in the perception and decoding of experience. Similarly, in the Buddhist tradition, identity is but a belief. The unity of a person is seen as merely a matter of continuity or causality in the succession of mental states or representations, such that "an element can be ascribed to a person if it is sufficiently closely related to other elements that have already been imputed" (Elster 1985). Given this similarity between Foucault and the Buddhist view, similar implications about identity can be drawn, albeit with a different emphasis:

> It is like watching a movie; the individual film frames are played so quickly that they generate the illusion of continual movement. So we build up an idea, a preconception, that self and other are solid and continuous. And once we have this idea, we manipulate our thoughts to confirm it and are afraid of any contrary evidence. It is this fear of exposure, this denial of impermanence, that imprisons us (Trungpa 1976).

Pirandello (1994) explores a related theme in his novella, *One, No One, One Hundred Thousand*, wherein his main character, Vitangelo Moscarda discovers that what he thinks he knows about himself is merely a consequence of perspective.

> *What are you doing?*—asked my wife, as I was indulging in front of the mirror.
> Nothing . . . just looking at my nose, inside this nostril . . . it hurts . . .
> *I thought you were looking at which side it leans to.*
> I turned as a dog whose tail had been stepped on.
> It leans? My nose?
> *Yes, darling! Look carefully; it leans to the right.*
> I was 28 and had always believed in having not a nice, but at least a decent nose (pp. 1–2).

In these first words, Vitangelo first comes to know, then falsifies, previous definitions of himself. Later (p. 77) he is queried:

> *Do you acknowledge that just a minute ago you were someone else? And you shouldn't be surprised! Ask yourself if you feel confident in saying that what you are today will last till tomorrow. This is the truth: they are self concepts in which you are stuck.*

In the end, Vitangelo concludes that:

> I did not know myself at all, I did not have a reality of my own, I was in a state of continuous fusion, almost fluid, malleable; others knew me, each in his own manner, according to the reality they had given me; they would see in me a Moscarda whom I wasn't, being nobody in particular for myself.

When Vitangelo starts looking at himself from the outside, fluidity is what he sees. Initially, the notion of a stable self is not a problem. Then, he discovers the selves that others are attributing to him and he starts the search for his "real self". In the end he realizes that this real inner self cannot be found, because it is not there. It is a work in progress.

Although we have represented the fluid character of individual identity in literary, rather than social theory terms, it is apparent that the malleability of identity is not confined to the macro level. Identity is difficult to define (at either the micro or macro levels). If we try to pin down a definition that emphasizes the stability of identity, we find that it constrains us in the face of necessary and essential flexibility. Of course, the assumption of *some* degree of endurance is necessary. We might then argue about the time length of its stability, but the notion of "lasting for some time" is nonetheless present. Our argument, however, casts that duration as often dramatically shorter than the currently employed treatments would have us believe.

The most important notion arising out of these preceding sections is that identity (and for our purposes, in particular, *organizational* identity) is more appropriately characterized as fluid rather than stable. It is necessarily changing more rapidly than the holders of that identity are inclined to acknowledge. In fact, taking into consideration the deep structure similarities between individual and organizational identity, we can also, in effect, work backwards from our social scientific observations about organizational identity and raise some interesting questions about the alleged endurance of individual identity, too.

Consider the parallels between experiencing personal and organizational identity. When I (my organization) trace(s) elements of my (our) identity to my (our) youth (founding), the same set of core values, orientations, and attributes seems to prevail. Thus, when I (we) look at myself (our organization), constancy is evident. On the other hand, other elements of my (our) values, orientations, and attributes clearly change over shorter periods of time, so that when I (we) assess who I (we) am (are) in this light, I see change. I (we) am (are) apparently both mutable and immutable. This little rhetorical experiment returns us to our paradoxical epigram: *Everything changes and nothing changes.* How can this be so?

## A FLUID IDENTITY WITH AN ENDURING PERCEPTION

There is a single overriding reason why identity is actually fluid and several major reasons why it is nonetheless perceived as enduring or stable.

### A Fluid Identity

Identity is fluid mainly because of its unavoidable and influential inter-relationship with image. As noted, identity is a product of social/environmental interaction. In prototypical form, that interaction proceeds as an initial presentation of a self-image (by an individual or an organization) and subsequent responses by other people, outside agents or competitors, who reflect an interpreted image back to the presenting person or organization. Identity is then constructed through comparison of self, presented, and reflected images, which can either affirm or subtly disconfirm the initial presentation. For organizations operating in diverse and rapidly changing environments, those reflected images can change rather quickly, affecting insiders' sense of how they are seen (their "construed external image"—See Dutton, Dukerich & Harquail 1994), and consequently, how they see themselves.

For instance, an organization might project an image as something it is not (e.g. high-tech company). A response ensues that this image is positive and very well received by some important constituency. Such feedback responses serve as an impetus for change (or at least the recognition of the need to change). Thus, organizations sometimes project tentative images to keep up with a moving target market, to which the market responds. In this fashion, images help to pull organizations into alignment with the demands and preferences of their environments (and thus to change identity to conform to desirable and workable images and actions). This example points up an interesting variation on the old folk observation, "Be careful what you ask for, you just might get it." In our case, the caution at the organizational level becomes, "Be careful how you project yourself, you just might become it." (See Gioia, Shultz & Corley 2000 for a detailed rendering of the process by which identity begins to change to conform to image over a relatively short time horizon.)

Reconsidering our opening question then, what constitutes a time horizon? Consider that American universities, and especially business schools, were rooted in the idea of stable identities as late as the mid-1980s, viewing themselves predominantly as organizations whose main role was to supply educated talent to industry. All the while, industry was experiencing unprecedented turbulence. Then, around 1990, business schools began to experience intense, externally generated pressure for accelerated change when *US News and World Report* and *Business Week* began to construct and publish business school rankings. Suddenly, image mattered. A lot. Changes quickly began to take place that were aimed at maintaining and improving rankings. Those changes soon began to affect identity (Elsbach & Kramer 1996). Consider the implications of the current question of whether business schools are becoming more like businesses and less like traditional educational institutions (and especially what it might mean that business schools now frequently refer to students—especially MBA students—as "customers"). One could make the argument that business school time horizons have shrunk considerably due to the alternating-year publications of *US News'* and *Business Week's* rankings and are now of the order of one year. Schools' identities are now heavily influenced by these rankings and image and reputation management have become major enterprises among the top 50 business schools.

## An Enduring Perception of Identity as Stable

Identity is perceived as stable in part because people and organizations are marvelous at engaging in revisionist history. When the perennial question of "who we are" arises, organization members not only depend on current perceptions (Ashforth & Mael 1996), but they also tend to revise their perceptions of the past to align with their current perceptions (cf. Loftus 1980). Due in large part to the strong interrelations between identity and image, the "facts" of the past are given up-to-date meaning, which contributes to the construction of a somewhat mythological history. The perceptual revision of history, therefore, makes fidelity to a previous conception of identity rather problematic and facilitates the fluidity of identity. Yet, the effort to maintain continuity with past understandings makes identity appear stable to organization members, even as it is changing.

Perhaps a more important reason that identity seems unchanging stems from the nature of labels. The essence of the observation here is straightforward, but revealing: *the labels used to describe facets of organizational identity are stable, but the meanings associated with those labels are variable.* The apparent durability of identity, therefore, is actually associated with the stability of the labels used by organization members to express who or what they believe the organization to be. Even though people might use the same labels to describe features of their identity, those elements are nonetheless subject to multiple and variable interpretations. This implies that identity changes with changing interpretations, which is the key feature of labels that allows members to live within the paradox that everything changes while nothing (appears to) change.

It is also important to recognize that the same label might have multiple workable meanings to two or more different organizational members, but that they are nonetheless able to agree that, "This is part of our identity in this organization." The robustness of the labels in accommodating many possible meanings is critically important to the development and maintenance of identity. Similarly, people outside the organization can more easily work with labels that have robustness. When investors identify a company as an "innovative company", this label resonates with the self-image of organization members. What precisely does "innovative" mean though? Innovative might mean that they consistently generate products that stay equal to and ahead of the market; it might also mean that they are taking reasonable risks to change with a changing world; it might also imply originality and daring, or it might simply mean adapting the tried and true to specific application. Such ambiguity allows a necessary flexibility. The implication of the robustness of labels is that organizational leaders should work to identify labels for core values that have great reach across internal and external constituents, such that all can agree on descriptive labels that have the flexibility to allow disparate interpretations and adaptability to changing conditions.

## SCATTERED IMAGES AND INDIVIDUAL IDENTITY

But this adaptive aspect of identity, and the ambiguity found in its labels, does not afford top management the freedom to manipulate images at will. Taking their cue from the realm of national politics, many organizations are finding themselves faced with a perceived need to practice spin as media scrutiny of the business world increases. Organizational spin can be thought of as a motivated attempt to manage interpretations surrounding ambiguous events or actions that might have negative consequences for the organization. While spin does not involve the projection of downright duplicitous images, it does present the occasion for discrepancies to arise between an organization's identity and the way it is presented to outsiders. Because there is often a strong link between organizational identity and individual identity, any perceived discrepancy in the relationship between organizational identity and image has the potential to influence individuals' sense of self as members of the organization. Images projected externally affect insiders.

As our whirlwind tour of the organizational identity literature illustrates, when an organization projects images about itself (conceivably as a reflection of its identity, but not always), those outside the organization refract images back to the organization that are subsequently picked up and interpreted by insiders. For as many external constituency groups that receive an organizationally projected image, there is the potential for an equal number of refracted images to be fed back to the members of the organization (Corley & Gioia 1999). In essence, organization members are faced with scattered images of their organization as they attempt to reconcile multiple images from multiple sources with their own conceptions of the organization (i.e. they make comparisons of identity with projected images and construed external images).

The scattered images notion leads to an interesting conundrum for our conception of individual identity within organizations—because organizations change their presentation of themselves in their attempts to manage external expectations and demands, conceptions of identity change as well (see Morsing (1999) for an extremely interesting example of this process). Thus, even if organizational identity *is* stable in the short term, and my personal identity within this organization is established and perceived to be stable because I identify with this organization every day, image projections are influential. If my organization is projecting images that do not match with who I think we are and, therefore, who I think I am, it raises questions and produces dissonance that affects the conception of identity.

This observation highlights the final aspect of the opening paradox. One reason we do not like our organizations to change too quickly is because that means *we* need to change too quickly. That is, if we can maintain some continuity in our identity as an organization, it is easier for me to maintain continuity in the conception of who I am as a member of the organization. People seek out organizations that are aligned with their values. If people cannot see the congruence or coherence between their beliefs and values and the images the organization projects of itself, then there are immediate implications for their identification with the organization and their identities as members of those organizations.

Therefore, we must also look at how individual identity changes as a consequence of being a member of an organization subject to the influences of images. As a result, we may find that we are not even able to conceive of individual identity in organizations as being as stable and enduring as we might like it to be. To exist within the paradox that is identity in modern-day organizations, relatively rapid change over time must be recognized and accepted as a natural part of the complexities of individual–organization–environment relations.

## CONCLUSION

We are accustomed to thinking of identity as enduring over long periods of time, of changing only grudgingly, of being dragged kicking and screaming into the twenty-first century. We seem to have maintained a fiction about the stability of identity when, in fact, reasonable consideration suggests that identity changes behind a façade of endurance. The notion that we retain stable labels while things change behind the scenes also applies to the character of theory and research over the last decade. We have acted as if the accepted definition is adequate. We have used and repeated it, even though the reported evidence seems to demonstrate that the assumed endurance of identity does not hold up to scrutiny (e.g. the classic Dutton & Dukerich (1991) study). Even the conversations in the last Sundance Conference all began with the accepted assumption of endurance, and then promptly proceeded to argue against endurance, without surrendering the label. Unlike the benefit of ambiguity at the practical level, however, at the theoretical level, the labeling of identity as "enduring" is not facilitative. Rather, it is a hindrance. It is important that we instead view identity as having *continuity in its malleability* as we pursue the high-potential trends in identity theory and research.

These trends should explore the temporal aspects of identity (at both individual and organizational levels) that hold good promise for providing additional insight into the relationship between identity and change. For instance, under what circumstances might change in identity have fast-cycle characteristics or slow-cycle characteristics? How does the notion of a temporal lag arising out of changes to organizational identity, the projected images based on that identity, or the resulting reputational feedback based upon those images influence traditional notions of alignment and fit, as well as the conception of identity as stable and enduring?

These trends should explore not only the fluidity of identity, but also the implications of projecting scattered images for organizations, as well as for the individuals who inhabit them. In addition we believe the coming explorations concerning identity will see trends oriented toward (1) a greater concern with *organizational* identity (rather than further extensions of individual identity conceptualizations to the organizational level); (2) identity and image as multi-level phenomena (see Rousseau (1985) and House, Rousseau & Thomas-Hunt (1995)); and finally (and perhaps surprisingly) (3) a trend away from the study of identity alone and toward the study of image (whether projected, refracted, or externally construed) and reputation, because ultimately, the story of identity in the modern and post-modern era is a story of the influence of image.

## REFERENCES

Albert, S. & Whetten, D. (1985) Organizational identity. In B. M. Staw & L. L. Cummings (Eds), *Research in Organizational Behavior* (Vol. 7; pp. 263–295). Greenwich, CT: JAI Press.

Ashforth, B. E. & Mael, F. (1989) Social identity theory and the organization. *Academy of Management Review*, **14**(1): 20–39.

Ashforth, B., & Mael, F. (1996) Organizational identity and strategy as a context for the individual. In J. A. C. Baum & J. E. Dutton (Eds). *Advances in Strategic Management*, vol. 13: 19–64. Greenwich, CT: JAI Press.

Beck, E. M. (Ed.) (1980) *Bartlett's Familiar Quotations*. Boston: Little, Brown & Co.

Collins, J. C. & Porras, J. I. (1994) *Built to Last*. New York: HarperBusiness.

Corley, K. G. & Gioia, D. A. (1999) Reconciling scattered images: the consequences of reputation management for insider audiences. Paper presented at the Third International Conference on Reputation, Identity, & Competitiveness. San Juan, Puerto Rico.

D'Aveni, R. A. (1994) *Hypercompetition: Managing the Dynamics of Strategic Maneuvering*. New York: Free Press.

Dutton, J. E. & Dukerich, J. M. (1991) Keeping an eye on the mirror: image and identity in organizational adaptation. *Academy of Management Journal*, **34**(3): 517–554.

Dutton, J. E., Dukerich, J. M. & Harquail, C. V. (1994) Organizational images and member identification. *Administrative Science Quarterly*, **39**(2): 239–263.

Elsbach, K. D. & Kramer, R. M. (1996) Members' responses to organizational identity threats: encountering and countering the *Business Week* rankings. *Administrative Science Quarterly*, **41**(3): 442–476.

Elster, J. (1985) *The Multiple Self*. Cambridge: Cambridge University Press.

Gioia, D. A. (1998) From individual to organizational identity. In D. Whetten & P. Godfrey (Eds). *Identity in Organizations: Developing Theory Through Conversations*; pp. 17–31. Thousand Oaks, CA: Sage.

Gioia, D. A. & Thomas, J. B. (1996) Identity, image, and issue interpretation: sensemaking during strategic change in academia. *Administrative Science Quarterly*, **41**(3): 370–403.

Gioia, D. A., Shultz, M. & Corley, K. G. (2000) Organizational identity, image and adaptive instability. *Academy of Management Review*, **25**(1): 63–81.

House, R., Rousseau, D. M. & Thomas-Hunt, M. (1995) The meso paradigm: a framework for the integration of micro and macro organizational behavior. In B. M. Staw & L. L. Cummings (Eds), *Research in Organizational Behavior* (Vol. 17; pp. 71–114). Greenwich, CT: JAI Press.

James, W. (1918) *The Principles of Psychology*. New York: H. Holt & Company.

Jick, T. D. (1992) *Managing Change: Cases and Concepts*. Burr Ridge: McGraw-Hill Higher Education.

Loftus, E. (1980) *Memory*. Reading, MA: Addison Wesley.

Luhmann, N. (1990) *Social Systems*. Bologna, Italy: Il Mulino.

Markus, H. & Nurius, P. (1986) Possible selves. *American Psychologist*, **41**: 954–969.

Martin, L. H., Gutman, H., & Hutton, P. (1988) Technologies of the Self: *A Seminar with Michael Foucault*. Amherst, MA: The University of Massachusetts Press.

Mischel, W. & Shoda, Y. (1995) A cognitive–affective system theory of personality: reconceptualizing situations, dispositions, dynamics, and invariance in personality structure. *Psychological Review*, **102**(2): 246–268.

Morsing, M. (1999) The media Boomerang: the media's role in changing identity by changing image. *Corporate Reputation Review*, **2**: 116–135.

Pirandello, L. (1994) *Uno, nessuno e centomila*. Milano: Newton Compton Editori.

Pratt, M. G. & Foreman, P. O. (2000) Classifying managerial responses to multiple organizational identities. *Academy of Management Review*, **25**(1):

Reger, R. K., Gustafson, L. T., Demarie, S. M. & Mullane, J. V. (1994) Reframing the organization: why implementing total quality is easier said than done. *Academy of Management Review*, **19**: 565–584.

Rousseau, D. M. (1985) Issues of level in organizational research: multi-level and cross-level perspectives. In B. M. Staw & L. L. Cummings (Eds), *Research in Organizational Behavior* (Vol. 7; pp. 1–37). Greenwich, CT: JAI.

Scheibe, K. E. (1995) *Self Studies: The Psychology of Self and Identity*. Westport, CT: Praeger.

Scott, S. G. & Lane, V. R. (2000) A stakeholder approach to organizational identity. *Academy of Management Review*, **25**(1): 43–62.

Tajfel, H. & Turner, J. C. (1985) The social identity theory of intergroup behavior. In S. Worchel & W. G. Austin (Eds), *Psychology of Intergroup Relations* (pp. 7–24). Chicago: Nelson-Hall.

Toffler, A. (1970) *Future Shock*. New York: Random House.

Trungpa, C. (1976) *The myth of liberty*. London: Shambala.

Whetten, D. A. & Godfrey, P. (Eds) (1998) *Identity in Organizations: Developing Theory Through Conversations*. Thousand Oaks, CA: Sage.

Whetten, D. A., Lewis, D. & Mischel, L. J. (1992) Towards an integrated model of organizational identity and member commitment. Paper presented at the Academy of Management, Las Vegas, NV.

# Index